THE FOUNDATION OF BRUNEL'S
GREAT WESTERN RAILWAY

GREAT WESTERN RAILWAY

BY

J.C. BOURNE.

THE FOUNDATION OF BRUNEL'S
GREAT WESTERN RAILWAY

André Gren

·RAILWAY HERITAGE·
from
The NOSTALGIA Collection

**This book is dedicated to Tony Moxon
and to Fiona, to both of whom I owe an enormous debt**

First published in 2003

British Library Cataloguing in Publication Data

A catalogue record for this book is available from the British Library.

ISBN 1 85794 210 8

Silver Link Publishing Ltd
The Trundle
Ringstead Road
Great Addington
Kettering
Northants NN14 4BW

Tel/Fax: 01536 330588
email: sales@nostalgiacollection.com
Website: www.nostalgiacollection.com

Printed and bound in Great Britain

Frontispiece **The frontispiece of J. C. Bourne's** ***The Great Western Railway.*** *Courtesy of Bristol County Record Office*

A Silver Link book
from
The NOSTALGIA *Collection*

A portrait of Isambard Kingdom Brunel by G. A. Sekon.

CONTENTS

ACKNOWLEDGEMENTS

N one of the many people on this list to whom collectively and individually I owe a great debt for all the help given me during the course of drafting this book will begrudge me beginning by paying special tribute to three people on whom I have made particularly heavy and frequent calls for assistance: Steve Priestley of the House of Commons, who has shown wonderful patience with me; Mike Stevens, who has participated in my research and made it much more fun; and Robert Harrison of the House of Lords Record Office, who has helped me unlock some marvellous source material for the book.

The Parliamentary aspects of the book have been improved by the help of three Clerks in the House of Commons, Jim Hastings, Andrew Kennon and Roger Willoughby. Dealing with my research and drafting has been helped by a number of computer experts, Paul Kummer, Brian Muligan, Harry Richards and Gareth Staton.

Great help with the illustrations was given by Elaine Seddon. Many debts are owed to the keepers of records relating to early railway history. These include Tim Bryan of 'Steam', Museum of the Great Western Railway at Swindon; Beverley Cole of the National Railway Museum, York, to whom I am particularly indebted for making me aware of the series of cartoons by Charles Saunders, which figures in my book; and archivists at the House of Lords Record Office and the Public Record Office, who have been unfailingly helpful.

Invaluable original material has been made available to me by the Earl of Carnarvon and his archivist, Jacky Lessware, and by the national firm of Bristol solicitors, Osborne Clarke. Good copies of the Bourne illustrations were helpfully provided by Mrs Bradley of Bristol County Record Office. Merton College, Oxford, has been most generous in making Select Committee records in particular accessible to me by financing the photocopying of them to be read on to tape by the Blind Readers' Service in the Bodleian Library, Oxford.

Any book of this sort needs to have thorough academic scrutiny to minimise the failings of the author. I have benefited by such assistance from Richard Griffiths, Sandra Jowett, Edward Olleson, John Prest, John Stevenson and Philip Waller. The errors that have survived their scrutiny are entirely my responsibility. The book has also benefitted from the exacting scrutiny of my editor, Will Adams. The Transport History Research Trust has been generous in providing funds to assist my research.

Reconciling poor vision with the appalling manuscript of many of the original sources for this book has been made possible by the untiring and uncomplaining help of Oxford University's Blind Readers' Service, in particular, Martin Davis and Kim Miller. Diana Everest, Peggy Ducker, John Sykes and Tony Ives helped with the proofs.

Lastly, I would single out two people who have given me great encouragement, acted as critical readers, and generally kept me going when I needed that kind of support. These are my wife, Fiona, and my late father-in-law, Tony Moxon. The extent of my debt to them both is such that I unhesitatingly dedicate this book to them.

EARLY RAILWAY HISTORY TIME-LINE

19 April 1821	Stockton & Darlington Railway incorporated
3 July 1821	George Stephenson appointed by the Liverpool & Manchester Railway
1 December 1821	Prospectus issued for a railway from Bristol to Bath
5 May 1826	Liverpool & Manchester Railway incorporated
6 October 1829	Rainhill Trials, won by Stephenson's *Rocket*
15 September 1830	Liverpool & Manchester Railway opened
17 March 1833	Committee of Inquiry into a Railroad from London to Bristol appoints Brunel to survey a route
6 May 1833	London & Birmingham Railway incorporated
30 July 1833	Bristol Committee of Inquiry reports
31 December 1833	Great Western Railway's prospectus published
20 February 1834	Bill for the 'divided route', London to Reading and Bath to Bristol, presented to Parliament
25 July 1834	Bill defeated in Lords by 47 votes to 30
25 February 1835	Bill for entire route presented
31 August 1835	Great Western Railway Act passed
14 September 1835	Brunel recommends Broad Gauge to his Board
27 May 1838	First train on the Great Western Railway from Paddington to Maidenhead
4 June 1838	First public service on the Great Western Railway
30 June 1841	Great Western Railway opens throughout

1.
GOD'S WONDERFUL RAILWAY: THE QUALITY OF BRUNEL'S GREAT WESTERN

'[Mr Brunel] has reduced all the inclinations… The levels are undoubtedly superior to any extensive line with which we are acquainted, and are therefore adapted to the working of locomotive engines, both as regards economy and expedition.'

George Stephenson, 31 March 1835

'I have looked for the perfection of the surface on which the carriages are to run as the great and ultimate desideratum.'

Isambard Kingdom Brunel, 26 January 1837

The proposed route of the Great Western Railway was set out in the 1833 prospectus: the line would be 114 miles long, from Bristol to a point of junction with the London & Birmingham Railway near Wormwood Scrubs. The station for passengers in London would be near the New Road, in the Parish of St Pancras. The railway would pass close to Southall Cattle Market, through West Drayton, within 2 miles of Uxbridge, near to Slough, Maidenhead and Wallingford, within 4 miles of Abingdon, and 10 of Oxford; the prospectus projected branches to both the latter places. The railway would then pass close to Swindon and Chippenham, from where two branches could communicate with Cirencester, Stroud, Gloucester and Cheltenham to the north, and with Melksham, Trowbridge, Bradford, Frome and Warminster to the south. The last part of the line would be through Bath to Bristol. The route is shown on the accompanying map. It is immediately obvious that a major distinction between the Great Western and earlier railways such as the Liverpool & Manchester (1830) and the London & Birmingham (1833) was that the railway was not passing through a heavily industrialised area of Great Britain. It is therefore little surprise that the Great Western came to draw the bulk of its income from passenger traffic rather than freight.

Therefore the breakdown between passenger and goods use was very different on the Great Western from other railways, especially those in the newly industrialising North of England. Thus on the Great Western, during the second half of 1839, only 4.5 per cent of receipts came from freight. By contrast, in the same period, more than two-thirds of the train journeys on the Liverpool & Manchester were by goods trains.

THE QUALITY OF BRUNEL'S ENGINEERING PROPOSALS

Quality was very close to Brunel's heart, and affected the costs and income of the Great

Western. The Company's Board members obviously lacked the technical knowledge to fully comprehend Brunel's engineering of the line, and expressed their misgivings to George Stephenson, who had, of course, pioneered railways in the North of England, and had engineered the world's first passenger railway, the Liverpool & Manchester Railway of 1830, for which the Rainhill Trials of steam engines had been held, and which he had won with *Rocket*. This fact obviously gave him considerable status in the eyes of railway promoters all over Great Britain, and the nervous promoters of the Great Western sought his views of Brunel's engineering proposals. He replied that Brunel had projected a line with levels superior to those on other railways with which he was acquainted.

George Stephenson appeared before the 1834 Committee on the Great Western Bill (as proposals for legislation are known before receiving Royal Assent and becoming Acts). He was asked if he thought that Brunel's estimate of the cost and income of the Great Western was 'a liberal one', to which he replied that he did, 'in every point of view'. Parliament's interest in – or wariness of – whether estimates were adequate to cover the cost of construction was the result of canal building. The most frequently recurrent and most intractable problem of canal finance had been that of raising additional funds to cover an increase in the cost of the works over the original estimate. Such an increase occurred in the case of every canal successfully completed, with only one exception, the Shropshire Canal.

Stephenson's reassurances to the Bristol promoters showed that Brunel was recognised as an outstanding civil engineer. His record as a locomotive engineer, however, was not good. This is shown by his espousal of the atmospheric system of propulsion on the South Devon Railway. On this system trains were propelled by a piston running in a tube between the rails. Robert Stephenson called it a 'rope of air', and his father described it as 'the greatest humbug in the world'.

The point is also confirmed by the unreliability of the engines that Brunel designed for the Great Western. Broad gauge engines were built for the Great Western by various builders, and their early inefficiency was reflected in the relative shortness of their working lives. Of the 23 engines the company had in 1840, nine ceased work within five years. The longest-lived, *Lion*, lasted 35 years. Stephenson's engines lasted more than 30 years, with the exception of *Dog Star*, which ceased work after only four years.

There were strong tensions between Brunel and Gooch resulting from Brunel losing the completeness of his control of every aspect of the Great Western to Gooch. Gooch's diary records a major weakness in Brunel, his style of running the Great Western. Gooch states that Brunel

> '…was reluctant to delegate any aspect of the work to others: one feature of Brunel's character (and it was one that gave him a great deal of extra and unnecessary work) was he fancied no one could do anything but himself.'

Evidence of this dominance is not hard to find: Brunel was responsible for the designs of Paddington and Bristol Temple Meads stations, the quality of which is brought out by the accompanying illustrations, and for the plans both of a station at Reading and much of the Railway Village in Swindon. He designed the bridge over the Thames between Maidenhead and Taplow, which was to form the subject of Turner's powerful painting *Rain, Steam and Speed* of 1843. Additionally, Brunel's biographer L. T. C. Rolt suggests that Brunel coined the name 'Great Western Railway' for what had formerly been described in Bristol newspaper reports as The 'Bristol & London Railway', and a flier issued by the company to encourage share

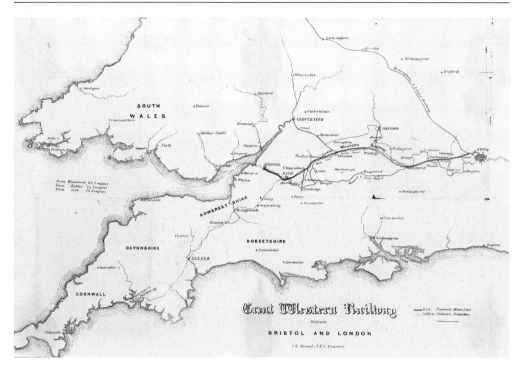

Above **Map of the Great Western Railway.** *GWR Museum, Swindon*

Below **A Bourne drawing of the locomotive facility at Bristol.** *Courtesy of Bristol County Record Office*

Above and below Brunel's passenger station at Bristol, the latter as drawn by Bourne.
Courtesy of Bristol County Record Office

ownership reinforces this observation. The new title came into use after the company's first Board meeting.

Brunel also initiated the absorption by lease of the Cheltenham & Great Western Union Railway in 1840, adopting a role that one might have expected a director of the Great Western to have more appropriately undertaken. Certainly, the Great Western's Board minutes covering negotiations for the absorption of the Bristol & Exeter Railway record that much of the negotiations were undertaken by Board members. However, the Great Western's Board minutes record that Brunel proposed the absorption of the C&GWUR because that company held land on which he wanted to build a station in Swindon for the Great Western, which was of 'mutual benefit' to both companies. The Great Western would pay all the Cheltenham's costs in creating a separate platform for that railway at Swindon. These negotiations show the extent of Brunel's control: no mention is made of the involvement of any Great Western director in the preparation of this arrangement. Yet a further illustration of Brunel's desire to be seen to be in charge of absolutely everything is shown in his involvement in drawing up the rule-book for engine drivers: one might have expected this task to have been left to Gooch in his capacity as Locomotive Superintendent. All these examples point to the extent and depth of Brunel's involvement in the establishment of the Great Western.

Cost was materially a major consideration for the promoters of railways, and the Great Western, per mile, was one of the most expensive railways in Britain. To some extent this was the result of the employment by the Board of Brunel as its engineer, who persuaded them that the engineering of the Great Western should be of a high standard. In addition to cost, Parliamentary Committees were also interested in the extent to which railways were disfiguring the landscape of Great Britain. Brunel was asked by the House of Commons Committee in 1834 whether, in selecting his route, 'has it been a part of your instructions from the company, and has it been your endeavour, so to arrange the line so as to injure ornamental property as little as possible?' to which he replied, 'Most particularly, and I was not only instructed to do so, but endeavoured to do so from the commencement, before I had regular instruction.' Brunel, characteristically, was reluctant to acknowledge any superintending control of his activities by his Board of Directors. Of course, given that the railway required land in two of Britain's largest urban centres, London and Bristol, it might be thought that ornamental property was of little consequence to the engineering of the Great Western, but Brunel's consideration on this question may well have been politically astute. The railway was one of Great Britain's longest, and went through a rich agricultural area.

Brunel itemised for the 1834 Commons Committee the splendour of his engineering proposals: between Bath and Bristol, the cost of cuttings and embankments, tunnels, masonry, rails, roads, fencing, depots, and locomotive power would total £965,760. The 1834 estimate was, of course, for the route from London to Reading and Bath to Bristol, not for the whole route. The equivalent at the beginning of the 21st century would be just over £56 million. Ultimately the Great Western was to cost £56,254 per mile, while the Eastern Counties Railway, at 126 miles the longest railway authorised at the date of incorporation in 1836, cost only £35,827 per mile.

Saunders told the 1839 Select Committee on Railways that Brunel had increased the embankments on the line compared to other railways in order to improve the gradients of the Great Western. One consequence was an increased requirement of land on either side of the line for those embankments, and William Sims, Chairman of the Great Western in succession to the first, Benjamin Shaw, told the same Committee that the Great Western had had to take 12 acres of land per mile instead of the originally projected 8 acres, which had been a major factor in the costs of construction over-running Brunel's estimates laid before Parliament in 1834 and 1835. The Great Western had therefore had 'a considerable increase on his estimate for earth-work'.

As has been seen above, George Stephenson acknowledged the advantages of the route Brunel had chosen, and confirmed for the promoters of the Great Western how favourable the inclinations on Brunel's selected line were. Brunel was asked by the Select Committee on the Great Western Bill on 24 March 1835 about the inclinations on his line compared with those of other railway companies. He replied:

'...referring to the London & Birmingham, the Birmingham & Liverpool, the London & Southampton and the Liverpool & Manchester, and the other principal railways, I believe there is no similar extent of country to be compared to that between London and Swindon for laying a railway.'

That statement gave little indication of his own abilities as a civil engineer.

Brunel was a perfectionist, who resented having to compromise his ideals to meet financial requirements such as making a profit. He wrote to the Board on 26 January 1837 that

'...in all the plans lately proposed, the object appears to be economy in first cost and neither durability or stability or perfection of construction appear to be considered of so much importance as the question of the cost and the details of construction.'

That Brunel was a perfectionist is also clear from the circular letter he sent to prospective manufacturers of engines and rolling-stock for the Great Western on 4 January 1836. He told them that all the materials and workmanship had to be of 'the best description' and 'similar to the same parts of the best engines now used on the Liverpool & Manchester Railway'.

Such evidence raises the question of whether the employment by the Board of Brunel, the perfectionist, doomed it to great expense. The Great Western's abovementioned cost per mile was not the most extravagant of the period. The Manchester & Birmingham Railway (1837) linked, like the Great Western, two of the country's greatest cities (neither suffering the decline of Bristol), and cost £60,968 per mile; this was largely a consequence of land costs in the densely populated cities at the termini. By contrast, another Brunel-engineered line, the Bristol & Exeter, cost only £19,066 per mile, one-third of his Great Western.

The advantages of the quality of the Great Western's route are plain from evidence given to the Gauge Commission in 1846, which examined the railway industry immediately after its first, and most crucial, stage of development. It tabulated the speed of express trains, and recorded those of the Great Western travelling at 46.7 miles per hour from Paddington to Didcot, and 45 from Didcot to Swindon. The London & South Western travelled at 35 to 40.6mph from London to Basingstoke, the London & Birmingham at 34.4mph from Coventry to Birmingham, and the Grand Junction at 35.1mph from Birmingham to Stafford. Brunel told the Commissioners that

'...looking to the speeds which I contemplated would be adopted on railways and the masses to be moved, it seemed to me that the whole of the machine was too small for the work to be done, and that it required that the parts should be on a scale more commensurate with the mass and the velocity to be attained.'

the scant regard the visionary has for penny-pinching. Nevertheless, his directors did indulge him, as can be seen from the accompanying illustration of the conspicuous entrance to Box Tunnel, the largest single piece of civil engineering on the line, other than the trackbed itself.

THE GREAT WESTERN'S PERFORMANCE

This general assessment of the quality of Brunel's engineering leads directly to the financial results of Brunel's engineering proposals. The Great Western was, of course, run as a business by its directors, not by Brunel. Their reports to proprietors' (shareholders') meetings reveal grounds for some satisfaction at the way the company was performing. Table 1 shows the development of the company in terms of passenger numbers, receipts and expenses, and profits over the five years from 1835 to 1840; the line opened for business only in 1838. By the second half of 1845, however, seven years after the opening (to Maidenhead), almost two-thirds of the company's receipts were gross profit, which provided much of the foundation for the company's expansion by acquisition of other companies.

Context for the company's performance is provided by other railways, which brings out the efficiency of Brunel's Great Western. The 1844 Select Committee on Railways set out statistics for the costs and income of what it called the 36 'principal passenger railways' in Great Britain. These statistics are based upon returns for 1842, and are therefore used here to demonstrate trends in the operation of railways that were founded in the 1830s. By the time this evidence was compiled, the incorporation of major new railways was no longer regularly occurring, and the railways founded in the 1830s were maturing. These railways had been incorporated with a collective share capital of £23,500,000 and loan-raising powers of £14,300,000 (present-day equivalents of £13,865,000,000 and £843,700,000). In 1842 their receipts were £4,400,000 and their expenditure £2,990,000, giving a margin of gross operating profit of 43.2 per cent. This gross profit figure was extremely large, and goes some way towards explaining the concern being expressed in, for example, William Galt's 1844 pamphlet on 'Railway Reform' at the level of profits railway companies were attaining. Galt gave evidence to Gladstone's 1844 Select Committee on Railways, from which sprang the President of the Board of Trade's plans to create some degree of state control of the railways.

For the proprietors of early railway companies a major concern was, however, the return

Half-year	Receipts	Expenses	Passengers	Profit
31.12.35	Nil	£4,322		-£4,322
30.6.36		£92,512		-£92,512
31.12.36		£258,470		-£258,470
30.6.37		£316,500		-£316,500
31.12.37		£650,074		-£650,074
30.6.38	£15,974	£578,592	£100,222	-£562,618
31.12.38	£37,314	£617,937	£264,644	-£580,623
30.6.39	£43,491	£479,334	£258,854	-£435,843
31.12.39	£65,006	£626,308	£347,642	-£561,302
30.6.40	£84,673	£742,640	£378,736	-£657,967
31.12.40	£337,152	£873,191	£645,181	-£536,039

Table 1: The Great Western Railway's performance, 1835-40

they achieved on their investments. Overall, in a period with virtually no inflation, this return was good. In 1842 the total paid-up share capital for all Great Britain's railways was £1.336 million, which was producing a net profit of 4.3 per cent at a time of virtually non-existent inflation. That return fuelled further investment by the original proprietors and by others.

The Sealed Register of the Great Western listed each separate occasion on which proprietors had bought shares, and records a number of instances of people who were impressed enough with the projections of the company's profitability to buy shares on a number of such occasions. Thus John D. Lewis of London, who described himself as a 'gentleman', bought 515 shares on 61 separate occasions. More humbly, a clerk in Penzance bought 32 shares on 14 occasions. Margaret Roskell, a Liverpool spinster, bought 109 shares on 19 occasions, and a Liverpool merchant of the same surname bought 112 shares on 20 occasions. Charles Tothill, a Bristol chemist, bought 222 shares on 14 occasions, and Edward Vines, a Reading gentleman, bought 127 shares, also on 14 occasions. William Ware, a Cork solicitor, bought 92 shares on 19 occasions, and Miss Bessy Woodhead, a Hollinsworth spinster, bought 155 shares on seven occasions. These shares were selling for £100 each, or a present-day equivalent of £5,900.

The Register was drawn up by Charles Saunders on 29 October 1835, and as the Great Western had only received its Royal Assent and thereby authority to sell shares on 31 August, the Register's list of multiple purchases demonstrates the depth of enthusiasm for the railway revolution among a substantial number of investors.

Railways were projected by their founders as a public benefit, but the principal motive of those investing in them, given that there was no state involvement in railway incorporation, was personal profit. The Great Western paid its first dividend to shareholders in 1840, and during the first half of the following decade dividends ranged from 3 to 8 per cent; those of the Liverpool & Manchester were 9.5 to 10 per cent, and those of the London & Birmingham were around 10 per cent per annum, a level that the Great Western did not equal during its first hundred years of operation, peaking at 8 per cent in 1845.

The good dividends being paid in 1841 by the Liverpool & Manchester added to the speculative excitement of the 'Railway Mania'. Investors in the railway companies were receiving in 1846 a return on their capital about double what was available from banks and the markets, and in addition, of course, the capital value of their shares was increasing: thus Liverpool & Manchester £100 shares were selling at £210 in October 1835, shortly after the incorporation of the Great Western, and fluctuated between £180 and £290 from January 1831 to December 1840.

According to a return drawn up by a firm of Leeds stockbrokers in 1841 of railway and canal shares, seven of the top 20 railway companies were worth less than their cost. However, the London & Birmingham, the most valuable, had cost £6,091,000 when opened in 1838, and was worth £13,378,000 in 1841. The Great Western, the second most valuable railway at the time, had cost £6,678,000 and was worth £8,390,000.

A more focused comparison between the performance of the Great Western and the

Liverpool & Manchester	10%
London & Birmingham	9.5%
Great Western	3%
North Midland	2%
Eastern Counties	1.75%

Table 2: Dividends paid by some principal railway companies in 1841

largest single railway company, the London & Birmingham, is of interest, and brings out the quality of Brunel's vision in practice. In the two years from January 1839 to December 1840 half-yearly passenger numbers on the London & Birmingham grew by 48.4 per cent. During the same period, the Great Western's passenger numbers grew by 249 per cent. On the London & Birmingham the number of miles travelled by passengers grew from 39,675,863 in 1839 to 47,606,450 in 1840. However, while the London & Birmingham was indeed the largest railway in capital terms when founded, its rate of expansion was dramatically lower than that of the Great Western: half-yearly receipts of all types, from passengers, goods, mails, etc, on the London & Birmingham grew by 150 per cent, those of the Great Western by 775 per cent. The receipts were not, however, reflected in the dividends the two companies paid their proprietors: those of the London & Birmingham did rather better than those of the Great Western. This is explained by the fact that the Great Western was putting most available receipts into expanding the company, not into paying dividends. That distinction is characteristic of Brunel's vision for the Great Western, allowing no compromise with distasteful realities such as showing a net profit for shareholders.

By 1846 money had moved into railways in a big way. A Parliamentary return showed that there were in Great Britain 126 men who had invested more than £100,000 in railway companies (£5,457,647 at today's prices). George Hudson held more than any other single individual, £818,450 in 12 schemes. Charles Russell was the only Great Western director who in 1846 held over £100,000 in railway shares, having £135,720. In contrast to how few very rich men there were among the Great Western's directors, 11 directors of the London & Birmingham then held more than £100,000 in railway shares. The Chairman of the Bristol & Exeter, a Great Western client company, Frederick Ricketts, a London merchant, had £217,650 in railway shares. The largest holding in Great Western shares of any of its directors was Robert Bright, who had bought 2,590 £100 shares in 1835. Nevertheless, under the terms of the Great Western's incorporation Act of 1835, to be a Great Western director a man had to have bought more than £2,000 in shares (£118,000 at today's prices). Thus while the Great Western's directors could not compete in terms of material wealth with those of the London & Birmingham, by no stretch of the imagination could they be described as having been poor. Still, the absence of such magnates and the relatively low priority given to dividends, certainly compared to other railways such as the Liverpool & Manchester and the London & Birmingham, helped clear the path for Brunel's total domination of the company.

The profits being drawn from railway shares were obviously affected by the costs of running railways. The London & Birmingham cost £242,067 to run in 1840. Of that total, just over a quarter was for maintenance and repairs of the track, a further quarter for locomotive power, and 23 per cent for coach traffic charges, including repairs. Receipts that year were £748,235, leaving a very good profit margin.

Table 3 gives a direct comparison of the London & Birmingham's costs and those of the Great Western. Most strikingly, the Great Western spent over one-third more on engine and carriage plant than did the London & Birmingham, for a broadly similar mileage. The revenue generated was also broadly parallel, which suggests that the Great Western offered passengers a better standard of accommodation. Given that, as has been seen, the London & Birmingham was producing a better return for its investors, the quality of the Great Western here shown is further evidence of the extent to which Brunel's ideals prevailed.

The table shows the quality of the Great Western. First and foremost the company had spent almost one-third more on rolling-stock than the London & Birmingham. The comparison for locomotive power shows that all this extra expenditure must have gone on carriages.

Costs	Ratio, GWR to L&BR
Engine and carriage plant	1 to 0.76
Repairs	1 to 1.01
Locomotive power	1 to 1.05
Passenger mileage	1 to 0.94
Passenger revenue	1 to 1.07
Average speeds	1 to 0.80

Table 3: Comparative running costs of the Great Western and the London & Birmingham

Passenger mileage was higher on the Great Western, but this was not reflected in the revenue generated. The foremost indication of the quality of Brunel's Great Western was that the average speed it attained was some 25 per cent higher than on the London & Birmingham. Passengers were therefore travelling at much higher speeds and in more comfortable coaches than on one of the Great Western's major rivals of the 1830s.

An analysis of working expenses as a proportion of receipts emphasises how favourable railways were for investors. The Great Western Railway was the most costly per route mile of the principal railways (that is, those with a capital of more than £2,500,000, as listed in Table 5, page 26). In 1842 expenses constituted 35.5 per cent of receipts. On the Eastern Counties the figure was more than 40 per cent. In 1840 the London & Birmingham's expenses were 32 per cent of receipts; in 1841 the figure was 28 per cent, and in 1842 25 per cent, leaving a very substantial margin of gross profit. The Great Western had cost significantly less to build than other major railways when measured against the receipts the line generated.

To produce such margins promoters had first to obtain the sanction of Parliament for their proposed line of railway. The character of the legislative sanction railway companies were seeking over the period to 1840 is well illustrated by the Great Western's legislation. Its parent Act was that of 1835, which set out the line's route, among other things, but the next Session the company put up a Bill to enable it to alter its route in the parish of Temple in Bristol, and in one parish in Gloucestershire, ten in Wiltshire, four in Berkshire, and six in Buckinghamshire.

In 1837 the Great Western Company brought forward another Bill, to gain access to Paddington, which received its Royal Assent on 3 July. The Great Western Company was to erect a bridge over the Grand Junction Canal at Paddington, and to make good roads it damaged there. In anticipation of the effect that the coming of the railway to Paddington might have, the Act banned 'foundry or other objectionable works or trades' on the Paddington Estate. The Great Western Company was to maintain the additional police that would be required (Charles Saunders was to capture police operations on the Great Western in practice in one of his cartoons, reproduced here). The Grand Junction Canal was protected, as was the Grand Junction Waterworks, and there was a clause to deal with the contamination of water. The Act set out the rates the Great Western Company could charge for carrying passengers and goods, and for wharfage.

In 1839 the Great Western Company was running short of money, and brought forward a Bill to amend its Acts, principally by raising a further sum of money, which received the Royal Assent on 4 June 1839. The Great Western was empowered to create new shares to the value of £1,250,000, and to raise a third of that sum on mortgage.

Some context for the Great Western's use of Parliament is provided by the Eastern

'The Constable on the Great Western Railway who was run over by the train whilst taking his tea': a satirical pen and ink sketch by 'C. A. S.', possibly Charles Alexander Saunders, c1840. *National Railway Museum, York*

Counties, which linked London and Great Yarmouth and put forward even more Bills in the years to 1840 than did the Great Western. As has been seen, the Great Western's first Act after its parent Act, the 1836 (No 1) Act, was to enlarge the powers it had been granted. Similarly, the second Eastern Counties Act, of 1836, gave it powers for 'altering and amending' the parent Act, and to build a new line. By its fourth Bill, in 1840, the Eastern Counties was seeking additional capital, but the Bill was withdrawn before it reached a second reading.

THE GREAT WESTERN AND RAILWAY INCORPORATION: AN OVER-VIEW

The Great Western's incorporation illustrates several themes of railway incorporation in the 1830s. It was a much bigger phenomenon than canal investment had been, involving larger sums of money, the incorporation of more companies, and many more investors. Parliament was suspicious of the whole process of railway incorporation, a suspicion of which Gladstone, at the Board of Trade, was to make much use when chairing the Select Committee on Railways in 1844 as the responsible minister, and also shortly afterwards in legislating to try to bring some Government control over this speculative mania. Railway incorporation constituted the first test for the post-Reform Act House of Commons, the franchise having been broadened under that Act of 1832.

This speculative mania, justly described as the first 'Railway Mania', drew in very many people in Great Britain, both as investors and as landowners who were to lose property to the compulsory purchase powers contained in railway incorporation Acts. Their private interests were being set aside for the sake of a greater 'public good' by a House of Commons that saw itself as responsible for a broader range of constituents than had been the case before the 1832 Reform Act.

Parliament was by no means a formality for the promoters of railways despite the frequent projection of schemes as being of public benefit. In the period to 1840 railway companies in the Great Western area (the companies that up to and at the Grouping of railways in 1923 were absorbed into the Great Western group) lost 14 of 47 Bills (30 per cent). Such a scale of loss was to remain a grim reality for railway promoters in that area: in the period to 1846 they lost a further 67 of 137 Bills (49 per cent).

The post-Reform Act House of Commons was taking on a new role for Parliament, one that encompassed new concepts such as the representation of voters. The result was the significant proportion of Bills that were unsuccessful: often landowners, as in the Great Western's case with Eton College, had ready access to the House of Lords to have their interests defended.

Parliament was not putting a brake on individual greed, as can be seen from the extent of George Hudson's shareholdings. However, in the Great Western Company no individual assumed a similar role to that of Hudson on the basis of the size of his investment, although the largest shareholding director, Robert Bright, did become Chairman of the Bristol Committee of the Great Western's Board, facilitating Brunel's domination of the Great Western. The railways also militated against the domination of individuals because of the number of shares they each tried to sell, many more than individual canals had done. Thus in the early 18th century Ralph Allen had been faced by a statute limiting shareholding in the Warwickshire Navigation Canal to one share each. He had therefore established control by selling some of the 12 shares to several different relatives. No railway companies had as few shares as canal companies, and this process of the spread of industrial wealth coincided interestingly with political democratisation.

The Great Western was even more broadly based than other railway companies. There was obviously no parallel to George Hudson's role, but, equally, there was no parallel to the number of very rich men that figured among the London & Birmingham's directors. That was good for Brunel's domination of the company.

The process of railway foundation was a completely new type of event on the political landscape of Great Britain in the 1830s, and this novelty was to lead to much consideration of parallels in the experiences of other countries in Europe. The 1839 Select Committee on Railways took a great interest in the experiences of railway incorporation elsewhere in Europe.

The new Great Western company of the early 1830s had two unique characteristics – the 'broad gauge' and the divided route – and both bore the stamp of Isambard Kingdom Brunel. Assisted by the absence of any significant financial interest among the Great Western's shareholders and directors, Brunel was able to give full rein to his vision of what became dubbed 'God's Wonderful Railway'. He – like all who worked for the company throughout its existence – thought the Great Western was indeed a wonderful railway. The evidence produced in this book confirms his perception.

George Hudson, from a portrait by Francis Grant. *City of York Art Gallery*

2.
RAILWAY INCORPORATION IN THE 1830s

'I should think a railway was a very great advantage indeed, particularly if an increased facility of conveyance was given to this intercourse between London and also between Manchester and York, I am quite certain that it would be a very great advantage indeed to all traders, particularly to the retail trader who generally buys his stock in the market, and who instead of buying four months consumption would then be enabled, from the facility of conveyance and the ready communication, to buy at two months, and thereby if he employed a capital of £10,000 the same capital would enable him to carry on the same business to the same extent to the same advantage, with a saving of capital – I should suppose – of a quarter or a third, and much more advantageously.'

George Hudson to the Select Committee on the
York & North Midland Railway Bill, 1836

The Great Western, like all railway companies, had to be founded by an Act of Parliament. The procedures of Parliament for the consideration of such Bills (as Acts are known before they gain Royal Assent) and the quantity of railway promotion in the 1830s provide essential background to the assessment of the foundation of Brunel's Great Western.

These Acts set out the amount of money the promoters were authorised to raise to establish their railways, and stipulated how many shares of what value could be issued. They set conditions on the operation of railways, set tolls for goods and passengers, and gave the power of compulsory purchase over the route of the promoters' line of railway. Particularly in this last respect, Acts of Parliament were very convenient for the promoters, in that they gave them all the compulsory purchase powers they needed, removing the need to take on individual landowners to reach negotiated settlements to buy their lands.

Promoters such as Isambard Kingdom Brunel and, in the North of England, George Hudson had to play a political game to reduce hostility to their proposals from landowners who would lose land under the compulsory purchase powers. They argued in their prospectuses and in Parliament that the 'private interests' of landowners had to be set aside to attain the greater public benefit of railway communication between locations. The Great Western Railway Company's first effort to obtain such an Act was defeated in the House of Lords in 1834, and the necessary authority did not come until the following year.

In 1834 the Great Western's promoters put up to Parliament a Bill for the 'divided route', that is a line from London to Reading and Bath to Bristol. It was disparagingly described in the

Houses of Parliament as a horse with no neck. This proposal was put forward because the promoters were having difficulty in raising the necessary finance to enable their Bill to go before the House of Commons, and it was thought that the income from particularly the London to Reading section would enable the company to realise what it called its 'sacred object', the entire route from London to Bristol.

This process in 1834, like so much of the early development of the Great Western, was handled by the company's engineer, Brunel. The Bill's fate in 1834 showed that while Brunel was a man of immense skill as an engineer, he had very little sense of how to be effective on the political stage of the Houses of Parliament. The importance of the role he played is emphasised throughout this book, and it is therefore of significance to gauge his personal reaction to the defeat of 1834. He was enraged by the defeat of the Great Western's incorporation Bill in the House of Lords, and when subsequently the House of Lords threw out the company's Oxford & Great Western Union Bill in 1837, he wrote to Thomas Osier, the Great Western's Bristol Secretary, that

> '...a new crotchet has come across some Lord's head... This utter wanton disregard of the interests of the parties waiting is really disgusting. The tyranny exercised is as great as it could be under the most despotic government, and the only answer that one gets to the strongest appeals is insult and ridicule. If I had not been a radical before, I should become one now.'

Brunel's rage demonstrates an important consequence of his impatience to reconcile the demands of building a railway with the need to function effectively on an entirely different level in the world of politics, a world that was changing dramatically after the production of a more representative House of Commons under the Reform Act of 1832. Brunel obviously had superior technical knowledge to the Bristol merchants who were the promoters of the company, but assumed a similar position to George Hudson in his companies in master-minding the development of the Great Western. Unfortunately, Brunel did not combine technical with political acumen, and his advice to his Board to adopt the 'divided route' in 1834 led directly to the defeat of the first Bill of incorporation.

Great Britain was gripped by a railway revolution during the 1830s. Ordinary people were becoming involved in the Industrial Revolution through the purchase of shares in the large number of new railway companies, and this revolution provided an early testing-ground for the political revolution of the post-1832 Parliamentary reform era, not least in relation to the number of Bills that were to incorporate or amend the powers of railway companies during the rest of that decade. Almost all of Great Britain's principal railway companies were incorporated during the 1830s, and these legislative proposals greatly affected people's daily lives. The assault on ordinary people by large-scale capitalist operations gave Members of Parliament the opportunity to give early evidence that the interests of their constituents were of great importance to them, in a way that had not been evident in the unreformed House of Commons.

The Great Western was founded amidst a widespread fever of speculative excitement of railway incorporation: between 1831 and 1840 2,021 miles of railways were authorised for the whole of Great Britain, with an aggregate capital of £49,544,600. Table 4 maps out the contours of that growth in railway legislation, of which the development of Great Western companies provides ample illustration. The Acts are both for new railways and to amend existing powers.

An overall view of the extent of the railway revolution can be found in the evidence taken by the Select Committee on Railways in 1844, at a time when railway incorporation had ceased

Year	Number of Acts	Capital authorised	Mileage authorised
1821-33	99	£1,769,700	375
1834	14	£2,059,500	143
1835	19	£4,588,300	206
1836	35	£21,723,700	872
1837	42	£10,581,200	367
1838	19	£1,085,000	7
1839	27	£6,181,900	51
1840	24	£1,555,300	0
Totals	279	£49,044,600	2,021

Table 4: Total railway capital and mileage, 1821-1840

and more established patterns of profitability and performance were emerging from Great Britain's railway companies. By 1844 120 different railway companies had been established in the United Kingdom, with a total share and loan capital of £90,112,800 (just over £5.3 billion at present-day prices).

The development of the role of Government under the pressure of the economic and population growth of the early 19th century led to much public debate over the promotion of public welfare, and whether this would best be promoted by unrestrained free enterprise or by a proactive Government, a debate that foreshadows similar debate over recent years. The Ministries of Peel and Gladstone served as a particular focus for this debate. The Great Western's incorporation illustrates the development of the relationship between Parliament and private interests set up to promote public welfare in the form of railway companies. Naturally, the bias of the discussion is towards Bristol and the Great Western rather than towards other parts of the country, which were also experiencing railway development in the 1830s.

The process of railway incorporation had begun with the Stockton & Darlington in 1821, followed by that of the Liverpool & Manchester on 5 May 1826. The Great Western Railway was incorporated in 1835, and by 1840 47 Bills had been put forward for 15 Great Western companies – that is, the Great Western and the companies absorbed by it before and at the time of the Grouping of railways under the Railways Act 1921.

Table 5 gives the basis on which railway companies have been selected to provide context for the Great Western's early history, and lists six companies that, in addition to the Great Western, had a share and loan capital of £2,000,000 or more on incorporation. Normally, two-thirds of the authorised capital consisted of shares, and one-third of loan-raising powers.

By 1844, when the railway revolution was coming to maturity and railway incorporation had ceased, these seven largest companies headed 118 railway companies, with an aggregate capital of £57,387,735 in joint stock and £21,638,582 in power to raise loans, a total of £79,026,317 (just over £4 billion at today's prices). The seven largest therefore had slightly less than 23 per cent of all railway capital in Great Britain, and it is therefore appropriate to use these companies to illustrate patterns in the developing and running of Great Britain's railways in the 1830s and subsequently.

The statistics contrast with the use of Parliament to promote canals during the 'Canal Mania'. The canal boom had begun in 1790, and was dead by 1797: it reached its peak in late 1792 and the early part of 1793, and was reflected in the legislation of 1793 and 1794. In the period 1789 to 1797 there were 53 Acts to incorporate new canals, with an aggregate capital of £8,779,850.

Bristol & Exeter	£2,000,000	
North Midland	£2,000,000	
Eastern Counties	£2,133,333	
London & Brighton	£2,400,000	
Manchester & Birmingham	£2,800,000	
Great Western	£3,333,333	
London & Birmingham	£3,333,333	
Total	**£17,999,999**	

Table 5: Railway companies capitalised at £2,000,000 or more in shares and loans on incorporation

Of this total, £13,500,000 consisted of shares, and £4,999,999 of loan-raising powers.

The reasons why railways so out-performed the canals are straightforward. They offered speed of communication, as well as security from pilferage. Hudson's quote at the start of this chapter also describes the contribution of railways to the Industrial Revolution in increasing the turnover of capital. Just as railways had suffered from the flexibility of road haulage in the 20th century, so they were far more flexible than canals: moreover, the railway network was considerably more extensive, and most towns of any size had a railway station.

By contrast to these large railway companies, the two smallest railways had a capital of only £10,000 each, the Bridgend Railway and the Stratford & Moreton Railway, both of which had been authorised in the 1820s. The 44 smallest companies had a share and loan capital of less than £100,000, which had been the original capital of the Stockton & Darlington, Great Britain's first railway company, in 1821.

Almost a third of the Bills proposing new railways were unsuccessful, demonstrating suspicion within society of the new phenomenon of railways and that Parliament could by no means be treated as a formality by railway promoters. A major city such as Oxford was not to get Royal Assent for a railway until 1843, at the third time of asking. The Great Western itself lost two of seven Bills during the 1830s, including its incorporation Bill of 1834. During the same period the London & Birmingham lost none of four Bills, and the Eastern Counties one of four.

Before the House of Commons debated any Bill to incorporate a railway, the promoters had to raise a subscription list pledging one half of the required capital; this list had to be deposited in the Private Bill Office of the House of Commons. The letterbook of the Great Western's London Secretary, Charles Saunders, from 1833 to 1835 is dominated by letters to William Tothill, the Bristol Secretary, about the task of raising capital. For example, on 29 October 1833 he wrote that

'...our directors are making some advances with subscriptions among their friends, and I hope soon to have a list from each given simultaneously with about 100 new shares.'

1834	1835	1836	1837	1838	1839	1840
4	8	11	41	21	7	Nil

Table 6: Legislative proposals by Great Western companies, 1834-40

The significance of railway legislation has been summarised by R. W. Kostal:

'...the acquisition of a private Act ... involved the grant of expropriative power. It also conferred corporate status and limited liability. But of equal importance was the aura of legitimacy and viability which a railway Act lent to a railway association in the eyes of potential investors.'

At the heart of the matter was the debate as to whether the public good could best be promoted by allowing 'private interests' free rein. If a railway was needed between two locations, a group of people would come forward to build it. The promotion of their own interests would therefore enhance the public good, and their profits obviously depended on both the cost of the construction of the railway and the income from it. Table 7 sets out those railways costing more than £1,000,000 to construct (figures rounded to the nearest whole pound). The actual capital cost of the eight principal railways ranged from £6,652,000 for Brunel's Great Western (fully 25 per cent more than the next most expensive railway, the London & Birmingham) down to £1,890,000 for the Manchester & Birmingham; the Liverpool & Manchester cost £1,515,900. However, in terms of cost per mile, the Great Western was the fourth most expensive of the principal railway companies, being twice the length of all three of those exceeding it in cost per mile.

One of the most significant expenses promoters had to bear was the cost of getting their Bills through Parliament. These costs included the expenses of all the witnesses called before the Select Committees and room hire, as well as incidental expenses. Such Parliamentary expenses did not occur elsewhere in Europe, and this factor contributed at least partially to the lower promotion and construction costs in the rest of Europe. The construction of railways in Belgium cost, in total, £6,406,476, about two-thirds of which was expended on land, at an average cost of £18,000 per mile. In Germany the costs averaged £11,000 to £13,000 per mile. In the United States of America there were 178 different railway companies, with a collective mileage of 9,321.5 miles. The average cost per mile of these companies was £4,800, in a range from £1,600 for railways completed in the State of Kentucky, to £10,800 for railways in the State of Rhode Island.

Robert Stephenson told the 1839 Select Committee on Railways that one consequence was that fares per passenger per mile in Belgium were only 59 per cent of the cost of travel on the

Table 7: The cost of the construction of Britain's principal railways

Railway	Length (miles)	Cost per mile
Eastern Counties	126	£35,827
Great Western	118.25	£56,300
Liverpool & Manchester	30.75	£51,000
London & Birmingham	112.25	£53,100
London & Brighton	46	£57,300
Manchester & Birmingham	31	£61,612
Manchester & Leeds	51	£59,800
North Midland	72.75	£45,800
Total (all railways)		**£58,513,600**

Liverpool & Manchester. Stephenson attributed this to the higher cost of construction: a labourer cost 50 per cent more in Britain, based on figures for the Liverpool & Manchester. It is important to observe at this point that the cost of construction of all French railways was only 70 per cent of that of the average for all English railway companies.

Obviously, one question was whether land prices were higher, given that land was such a major component of the cost of establishing a railway. In Great Britain land represented 13.5 per cent of the cost of setting up the London & Birmingham, and 12.5 per cent in the case of the Great Western. The Committee quoted the Belgian Minister of Works, who had observed that the lower cost of Belgian railways could not be attributed to the lines crossing an easier geography. Equally, the 1844 Committee observed that the difference in expense could not be attributed to superior efficiency.

Nevertheless, the Committee then curiously cited evidence that suggested that the cost of constructing railways in this country was indeed substantially greater than in Belgium. There, land and compensation had cost £2,750 per mile, while the Great Western had paid £6,300 per mile. The cost of works and stations per mile was £10,600 in Belgium and £40,000 on the Great Western. As already mentioned, Parliamentary expenses were not paid in Belgium or France at all, and the costs in those countries of engineering, etc, were commonly at least half of those in Great Britain. The effect of these additional costs in Great Britain was that railway companies had to raise more money, and therefore had more shares, than their counterparts elsewhere in Europe. The profits thus had to be divided between a greater number of proprietors.

The Committee then analysed the causes of the extra expense. Station accommodation was £2,000 per mile greater in England, which was accounted for by the 'more ample and expensive' nature of the stations the companies wanted to build. The Committee blamed Parliamentary expenses, which averaged £700 per mile over the whole of Great Britain and did not arise in Belgium at all. Law charges (the cost of solicitors and court fees) averaged £1,000 a mile more in this country than in Belgium, which the Committee attributed partly to the nature of legal deeds, and to the higher rate of professional emolument. Land and compensation was approximately double the cost in Belgium: £6,300 per mile on the Great Western compared to £2,750 in Belgium. Lastly, the Committee cited 'extraordinary expenditure', which it attributed to the 'want of economy' only to be expected from the nature of joint-stock companies, which were managing 'expensive and complicated' businesses on a scale not previously experienced.

Railways in Britain and abroad also operated under different tax regimes. The 1844 Select Committee on Railways observed that

> '...it is material to observe that in this country what is called the high-fare system ordinarily prevails over the average charge of railway communication; a charge falling in no inconsiderable degree on trade and commerce, is very much higher than in other countries, where railways have been established; and that there is no clear or early prospect of a general reduction of the rate of charge under the present system of independent companies.'

The Great Western typifies the overall annual level of the costs of construction of Great Britain's railways. Its costs were shown in the directors' report to the proprietors of 1843, after the line had opened throughout in 1841. The first train had been from Paddington to Maidenhead, on 27 May 1838, and the magazine produced by the Great Western in 1935 to mark the centenary of its incorporation carried a portrait of Jim Hurst, who drove the first train from London to Maidenhead with a satisfied complement of directors as his passengers. The first public service followed soon after, on 4 June 1838. The statistics reveal clearly the pattern of expenditure peaking in the years of the main construction work, in the late 1830s. Half-yearly expenditure over the period to the end of 1842 peaked at £650,074 in the first six months of 1837. Calls on shares produced £3,033,758, and receipts from traffic were £1,466,092 in total. The directors' report records that over the six months to 31 December 1842 the company had received £283,942 from passengers, and a mere £75,682 from merchandise and parcels. The result of this income was a balance of profit for the six months to 31 December 1842 of £359,376.

The evidence taken by the Select Committee on Railways in 1839 confirms this analysis of the differences between costs in Great Britain and elsewhere in Europe. It took evidence from the directors of railway

Jim Hurst, driver of the Great Western's first train, from Paddington to Maidenhead.
GWR Museum, Swindon

companies deprecating this disproportion, and it is reasonable to assume that their concerns had been fed by dissatisfaction among their shareholders.

The main distinguishing feature of the Great Western amongst Great Britain's other railway companies was the use of the broad gauge of 7 feet instead of the 'narrow' gauge of 4ft 8½in. Brunel suggested this to the Board in his report of 14 September 1835. Early railway Acts did not specify the gauge of railways, and there is no mention of Brunel's thoughts on the matter in any of his reports before that date. His recommendation is reproduced in Appendix 3. Brunel told his Board that for a given consumption of fuel the same size of train would go further and faster on the broad than the narrow gauge. Brunel's visionary zeal is demonstrated in one of his first reports to his Board. He told it that in designing the Great Western he had '…always contemplated introducing all the perfection of materials and workmanship of which it is capable'. He acknowledged that his ideals added some £500 per mile to the cost of construction, but assured the directors that the excess would be 'amply repaid in the first few years of working'.

In 1846 the Gauge Commission conducted the first public assessment of whether the country should have a common gauge of railways. Brunel was asked by the Commissioners whether he would like to be able to have reversed his recommendation of the broad gauge. He replied that he would have favoured an even broader gauge than the 7 feet adopted by the Board on his recommendation.

1840 is a good limit to this review of the foundation of the Great Western and other railways for four reasons. First, all major British railway companies other than the Great Central had been incorporated by 1840, which was the first year since the incorporation of the

Liverpool & Manchester in 1826 in which no proposals for new railways came before Parliament. Second, 1840 was the first year in which the Great Western paid a dividend (1.5 per cent). Third, it was a year in which the form of the Great Western altered significantly when three companies were leased and the Great Western Company took over the full operation of the Bristol & Exeter, the Cheltenham & Great Western and the Oxford Railway Companies. The Bristol & Exeter was the largest single railway company in terms of capital that the Great Western absorbed throughout the 19th century. Fourth, 1840 was the first year in which the level of receipts projected in the report of the Bristol Committee in 1833 was attained and exceeded.

The development of railways in the 1830s produced an interaction of four groups, in a drama played out on the stage of the Houses of Parliament. These groups were, first, those lobbying for railways, such as George Hudson, the promoter of extensive lines of railways in the North of England, and Isambard Kingdom Brunel, the engineer of the Great Western and a large number of other companies; second, shareholders hoping to make a substantial and often quick return on their investment; third, the 'private interests' affected by the development, such as landowners; and fourth, Parliament, in reaction to the huge new demands placed upon its procedures by the quantity of railway legislation.

A major factor in the level of public interest in the phenomenon of railways, shown by the number of Select Committee inquiries into both Parliament's handling of the volume of railway legislation in the 1830s and also into the profits railways were generating for investors, was the level of that profitability, a level dramatically greater than had been experienced with canals. Greater levels of share ownership meant that there was a more widely based involvement by the general public than there had been in factories or mills. The latter had tended to be dominated by the families of the original developers, while promoters of canals had themselves been heavy investors in their undertakings. For example, the Avon Navigation had only 32 proprietors in all, and, as mentioned above, the chief promoter, Ralph Allen, was faced by a statute limiting proprietors to a single share each, so established control by buying shares in the names of seven relatives. By contrast, the Great Western had 1,443 shareholders, with no single individual having a dominating financial interest, although this was not widespread among railway companies – the Pease family dominated the Stockton & Darlington, and George Hudson controlled a substantial mileage of railways.

Railway companies in general were very profitable. As we have seen, the costs of the Great Western were greater than many other railways, due principally to the cost per acre of the land it had to buy between London and Bristol; the employment of Isambard Kingdom Brunel was another important additional contributory factor to this high cost, and is one consequence of Brunel's direct, personal role in the Great Western's relations with Parliament. However, this was very important given the number of Bills the company put through Parliament, certainly compared to other railway companies.

The profitability of railways led Parliament to consider taking them into public ownership. Such a level of profits was a new phenomenon in Great Britain, where wealth had formerly been accrued through land, while early industrial wealth had centred upon owners. The question of public ownership led to the Railways Act of 1844, after Gladstone's 1844 Select Committee.

3.
THE PROMOTION OF THE GREAT WESTERN

'The traffic from passengers on the line is proved to be greater than any other of similar extent in this country. The advantages of the commercial ports at each end, with an intermediate manufacturing district depending upon supplies of coal and raw produce from places connected with the railway are important features in the undertaking. Ireland and South Wales will largely contribute to the traffic through Bristol, while the much-frequented towns of Bath, Cheltenham and Oxford, in addition to the beautiful scenery of Clifton, Reading, Maidenhead and Windsor, cannot fail to attract an increasing number of passengers to the projected railway. The line may hereafter be extended through Devonshire, and form a main trunk of communication from the Metropolis to the West and South-West of England.'

Great Western prospectus, 1835

The first proposal for a locomotive-drawn railway emerged in Bristol in 1821, put forward as a 'Bristol & London Railway', at an estimated cost of about £8,000 per mile. The route proposed was to be covered by passenger trains at 12 miles per hour and goods trains at 8 miles per hour. Although Bristol showed an early interest in horse-drawn railways, it was the Stockton & Darlington, the first railway to be operated by locomotive traction, that received its Royal Assent on 19 April 1821. George Stephenson was appointed Engineer to the proposed Liverpool & Manchester Railway on 3 July 1826, shortly after that railway had received its Royal Assent, on 5 May. The Rainhill Trials were held in 1829, to assist the directors of the Liverpool & Manchester in determining whether to use stationary or locomotive engines on their railway, in the course of which *Rocket* emerged as the best locomotive.

Thus the main railway developments were taking place in the North East of England. The Stockton & Darlington line of 1825 proved the efficacy of the steam locomotive, and five years later the opening of the Liverpool & Manchester line proved the success of railways. Bristol, as one of the three major Atlantic ports, decided that it had to have its own railway to London, and what became the Great Western was founded after discussions between Bristol merchants subsequent to the opening of the Stockton & Darlington, at a meeting held in Bristol at the 'London Tavern' on 27 December 1831. The road engineer McAdam was employed as engineer, and he produced a plan in less than a fortnight. Curiously, he described the Cotswold Ridge as 'a small swell of the country near Dodington', which leads MacDermot, the foremost historian of the Great Western, to assume that he took no levels. However, no application to Parliament was ever made, and the project died a natural death.

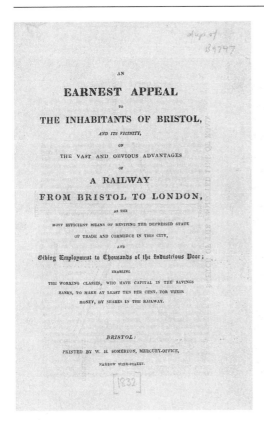

'An Earnest Appeal' to Bristol inhabitants to support the Bristol & London Railway, 1832.
GWR Museum, Swindon

In the same year schemes for 'The General Junction Railroad' from London to Bristol, the 'London & Reading Railroad', the 'Bristol Northern & Western Railway' and the 'Taunton & Grand Western Railroad' were put forward, but no record appears to exist of the causes of their ultimate demise. In 1832 the 'Bristol & London Railway' was projected, and the publicity sheet for that project is reproduced here.

Bristol was in danger of being completely eclipsed by the northern cities during the early part of the 19th century. The city had been Great Britain's second city during the 17th century, a position built on the slave trade principally with the United States. The loss of that trade and the development of industry, especially in the North of England, was felt acutely by businessmen in Bristol, and the urge to restore Bristol's position was a major factor motivating interest in a railway to London.

That Bristol's decline as a port was not arrested by the Great Western, as some of its promoters had hoped, emerged later from figures given by Samuel Laing, the Law and Corresponding Clerk of the Board of Trade serving as Secretary of the Railways Department, to a Select Committee. His figures, shown in Table 8, show the level of freight usage of 'the principal railways' for the half-year ending 30 June 1842, and it is evident that the Great Western was not one of the principal freight carriers in the country during that period.

A Committee of Inquiry was established in early 1833 to investigate the railroad, and a subsequent public meeting was held in Bristol on 30 March, resulting in the plan for the 'Bristol & London railway'. The 'numerous and respectable' meeting established a Committee, consisting of various Bristol interests to investigate further the proposal for the railway. It

Railway	Tons of freight carried (percentage of L&MR)
Liverpool & Manchester	87,000 (100)
North Midland	69,000 (93)
Manchester & Leeds	61,600 (85)
London & Birmingham	60,400 (69)
Great Western	42,200 (49)
Grand Junction	35,700 (41)
London & South Western	14,500 (17)

Table 8: Freight carried on the 'principal' railways, half-year to 30 June 1842

appointed three bankers (Miles, Harford & Co, Elton & Nailee, and Stuckey & Co), and set the cost of the undertaking at £2,540,600. A detailed exposition of this estimate is given in Table 9. The meeting was chaired by Robert Bright, a Bristol merchant who was to become the largest single shareholding director of the Great Western, with 259 shares (£25,900), and ultimately became the company's Deputy Chairman. He chaired the meeting because the Mayor of Bristol was ill; at a similar meeting to inaugurate the York & North Midland Railway, York's Mayor took the chair, evidence of the local importance of early railways.

The success of the Stockton & Darlington and Liverpool & Manchester Railways, which was shown by the increase in the value of their shares threefold and twofold respectively, was attractive to businessmen in Bristol, and the Committee reported on 30 July 1833 to a meeting of the inhabitants of Bristol and its neighbourhood. When Brunel had completed his survey of possible routes, the Committee congratulated itself that he had produced 'the proofs which it would be necessary to adduce before Parliament, in such a manner as to enable the Subscribers to present it with entire confidence in a complete and satisfactory state.'

THE 'DIVIDED ROUTE'

The Great Western's directors were concerned about the prospect of raising sufficient capital to enable them to proceed with their Bill in Parliament, and accordingly directed Brunel on 18 October 1833 to 'discontinue his survey between Reading and Bath, and to confine all further future expenses to the survey on the two extremities of the line'. The Board nevertheless determined to apply for powers in the subsequent Session of Parliament to build the intermediate section, adopting this course in order to complete the line at 'the earliest practicable opportunity'.

Although much concern was expressed in both Houses of Parliament over the 'divided route', the railway was described by its promoters as a Bristol to London Railway from its inception, and was headlined as such in the *Bristol Gazette*'s report of the 1833 Committee's meeting. On 1 August 1833 the paper reported that the projected level of receipts from passengers per annum was £747,754. In fact, in the first full year of operation over the whole route from London to Bristol the company recorded receipts of £551,099.

Charles Ludlow Walker, Mayor of Bristol and a member of the Bristol Committee of the company as a representative of the Bristol Municipal Corporation, told the House of Lords Committee on the Bill in 1835 that 90 per cent of firms approached about the desirability of the railway had approved it, and it had been brought forward 'certainly as a public measure; not as a matter of speculation'. Similarly, George Hudson had told the Parliamentary Committee on the York & North Midland that a public meeting to consider the establishment of that railway had been attended by almost 'the whole' of the 'principal inhabitants' of York.

A further prospectus was produced on 31 December 1833, which proposed a company capitalised at £500,000 in £100 shares. That prospectus was superseded by another that set the capital to be raised at a much more realistic level of £3,000,000, and set out an account of the likely costs of construction, as detailed in Table 9. By way of comparison, the Liverpool & Manchester Railway was completed in 1830 at a cost of £24,000 a mile, as detailed in Table 10; unfortunately, unlike for the Great Western, figures are not available for the Liverpool & Manchester for the projected cost of locomotives, nor are station costs separately identified.

Ultimately the Great Western was authorised by its 1835 Act of Incorporation to raise £2,500,000, very near to this projected level of expenditure. Some important distinctions can be observed between the projected costs of these two railways. First, and most evidently, although both linked two of Great Britain's major cities, the Great Western was projected to

Parliamentary, 'preliminary expenses'	£50,000 (2.0%)
Purchase of land, including compensation	£340,000 (13.4%)
Depots at London, Bristol, Bath	£223,000 (8.7%)
Bridges and masonry	£474,800 (18.9%)
Excavations, embankments, and tunnels	£835,300 (32.9%)
Rails, &c, laying and making road, &c	£520,700 (20.5%)
Minor depots and stopping places	£13,300 (0.5%)
Lighting tunnels	£5,000 (0.2%)
Locomotive power, including water stations	£78,500 (2.8%)
Total	**£2,530,600**

Table 9: Projected costs of the railway from Bristol to London, 1833

Cuttings and embankments	£199,783 (27%)
Chat Moss	£27,719 (3.7%)
Tunnels	£47,789 (6.5%)
Land	£95,805 (13%)
Fencing	£10,202 (1.4%)
Bridges	£99,965 (13.5%)
Formation of road	£20,568 (2.8%)
Laying of blocks and sleepers	£20,520 (2.8%)
Rails (£12 10s per ton)	£60,912 (8.2%)
Surveying, law, Parliamentary and incidental	£157,341 (21.2%)
Total	**£740,604**

Table 10: Projected costs of the Liverpool & Manchester Railway, 1830

cost more than three times as much in total than the Liverpool & Manchester. This was despite the land acquired by the Great Western costing only one-third of that for the Liverpool & Manchester. Engineering on the latter (cuttings and embankments, Chat Moss, tunnels, fencing, bridges, formation of the trackbed, blocks and sleepers) constituted 49.5 per cent of the total cost, whereas on the Great Western civil engineering (entrances into London, Bristol and Bath, bridges and masonry, excavations, rails, minor depots and lighting tunnels) represented 89.7 per cent of the total cost. Thus the Great Western spent 81 per cent more on civil engineering than the Liverpool & Manchester as a proportion of overall expenditure. Small wonder, then, that Brunel produced 'God's Wonderful Railway', albeit at a price.

Table 9 shows how misleading it is to view the Great Western's history chiefly from the standpoint of locomotives rather than (additionally, of course) its experience in Parliament: the former cost £78,500, compared with £390,000 for 'preliminary expenses' and 'land and compensation'.

THE GREAT WESTERN PROSPECTUSES

The first stage of the promotion to the public of the new company was the prospectus, an important marketing tool that projected the Great Western's costs and income. Its importance was such that it went through several drafts before being finalised. Two prospectuses were issued in 1833 and one on 18 August 1834. It was by no means unprecedented for a proposal for private legislation to go through several stages, in this case prospectuses, before gaining Royal Assent. For example, four Bills were put forward to establish navigation between Bristol and London immediately after the Restoration in 1660, including one proposal by the Earl of Bridgewater in 1668.

A major feature of the Great Western's first prospectus was the 'divided route', from Bristol to Bath and from Reading to London, which was a major factor in the defeat of the 1834 Bill of Incorporation in the House of Lords. The promoters had been having some difficulty in raising the portion of the capital required by Parliament as a deposit before a Bill could go forward, and Brunel first proposed to the Board that it should adopt the divided route, because the capital requirement would obviously be lower, and the income from the two sections of line would generate the resources to apply to Parliament for powers to build the complete line. When the directors sent a circular to shareholders after the defeat of the Bill in 1834 they described the completion of the line as their 'sacred object'.

The prospectus produced by the company dated 31 December 1833 said that traffic on the line would be greater than on any line of similar extent in Great Britain. It would benefit from having commercial ports at either end, with 'intermediate manufacturing districts' that relied on raw produce from places connected with the railway. The prospectus made clear the benefits the railway would gain from passenger traffic, singling out the 'much-frequented' towns of Bath, Cheltenham, Windsor and Oxford. The prospectus asserted that these could not 'fail to attract an increasing number of passengers to the projected railway'.

The Stamp Office was responsible for levying duty on stage coach travel, and its returns gave good statistics for the movement of people around the country. These returns were much used by the promoters of railways to justify their projections of income from their proposed lines. Thus Charles Saunders told the House of Commons Committee on the Great Western Bill on 23 June 1835 that calculations based upon Stamp Office returns and other sources showed that the Great Western would achieve an income from passengers and goods of £415,640. This figure was indeed achieved in 1840, although the complete line only opened on 30 June 1841. Passengers would be a major plank of income for the Great Western, and the prospective levels of such income were of great interest to Parliamentary Committees. William Shearman of the Stamp Office appeared before the Select Committees on different railways five times in all, once in 1834, once in 1835 and three times in 1836. His colleague in the Stamp Office, William Sutherland, appeared 14 times between 1834 and 1844.

One of Sutherland's appearances was before the 1835 Committee on the Great Western Bill, and he offered figures for coach journeys between London and places the railway would serve. The small number of journeys being made in comparison to levels of travel to be achieved on the Great Western Railway demonstrates the strength of one of the main arguments used by the promoters of railways, that there was a demand that was not being met, partly because of the cost of coach journeys, partly because of their lack of comfort for passengers (and horses), and partly because of the poor security they offered to goods traffic. He told the Committee of the number of coaches making journeys each week between London and various locations in the West. For example, 20 coaches were making a total of 136 journeys a week from London to Bristol, while four were making a total of 24 journeys a week to Cheltenham. Figures for 20 other routes added 615 journeys from London to other locations in the West of England, the largest numbers of journeys being 80 to Reading, 82 to Uxbridge, and 96 to Windsor.

In fact, a much higher increase in the levels of travel than those projected was achieved. The London to Maidenhead section opened in the second half of 1838, and carried 264,664 passengers during that period. Figures for the following years showed that Brunel's and Saunders's estimates had been by no means overly optimistic – passenger numbers grew from 364,855 in 1838 to 1,022,917 in 1840.

Obviously, during the period covered by this book, encompassing the Great Western's incorporation and construction, the company did not turn in a profit. It began to show a gross profit from the first half of 1842 (£157,678), which increased to £643,542 in the whole of 1845.

These figures per annum were greater than those recorded for the Liverpool & Manchester in its first three years of operation. A critical difference from the receipts profiles of the two companies can be observed from those the Liverpool & Manchester for 1835, when its total receipts were £217,480, of which 41.8 per cent came from the carriage of goods, a significantly higher proportion than on the Great Western. This was reflected in Parliament when the surveyor of the Great Western told the House of Lords Select Committee on the Great Western Bill in 1835 that the largest point of manufacturing on the line of the Great Western was Stroud.

The Stockton & Darlington, like the Great Western, exceeded initial projections in its results. Estimated revenue from that line was £16,209, all from the carriage of coals and merchandise, yet in its second year of operation, to 30 June 1827, revenue was £18,304. The quantities of coal carried and hence receipts rose each year, from £7,985 in 1825-6 to £57,819 in 1832-33.

The critical feature of Brunel's estimate was the cost of the line, which came to £2,540,600, including engineering works and rolling-stock, as well as the costs of 'Parliamentary and other preliminary expenses' (see Table 9 above). The projected annual income from passengers and goods was, as we have seen, £415,640. The members of the Bristol Committee of 1833 (the Committee set up in Bristol to consider the desirability of establishing a rail link to London, and which had appointed Brunel to survey a route) demonstrated the strength of their conviction of the 'great advantage' by personally investing in the undertaking. The subscriptions of the 13 Committee members are set out in Table 11 below, and totalled £201,200 (almost £12,000,000 at present-day prices). The company's projected income in the 1833 Committee's Report was £747,754 per annum from passengers alone, yet the level achieved from passengers in the line's first full year of operation – 1839 – was £726,378, and that over only part of the route from Bristol to London, the whole route not opening until 1841.

Promoters of other railways were also asked by their Parliamentary Committees about the predicted traffic and invariably gave figures for stage coach travel on the proposed route, yet a much higher increase in the levels of travel than that projected was achieved. The Great Western's success after its opening is shown by the increase in passenger figures from 606,396 in 1839 to 2,441,255 in 1845. Equally, the surplus of income over expenditure increased from £146,678 in the first half of 1842 to £293,696 in the second half of 1845.

The local background but national significance of the undertaking was much emphasised by the company in its promotion. A letter sent out to prospective subscribers in October 1833 stated that:

'...the project is not a private speculation by a few private individuals, but the result of nearly twelve months careful investigation by a Committee consisting of the Deputies appointed for that purpose by the Municipal Corporation and the other public bodies of this City [Bristol]. The scheme had therefore been proposed because it would not only be of the greatest ... utility as a work of national importance but affords an ample return of profit. Revenue would certainly exceed projections.'

Another Great Western prospectus followed, and estimated the cost at £8,000 per mile (£447,000 at present-day prices) for a line 60 feet wide, including rolling-stock and 'every other charge'. As we have already seen, the cost was to rise to £56,300 per mile by 1844, a total of £6,657,475, and only three railways cost more per mile, the Manchester & Birmingham, the Manchester & Leeds (which ran over a far more difficult country than did the Great Western) and the London & Brighton, the latter being about half the length of the Great Western. The cheapest of the major lines were the London & South Western, at £27,800 per mile, and the Grand Junction, at £23,200.

The first report of the Great Western's directors to the proprietors, on 29 October 1835, showed that the company had spent £18,168 on engineering, including surveyors, land valuers, and what were described as 'professional witnesses' in Parliament, and a further £38,772 on solicitors, fees to counsel, and other law charges and disbursements, while £8,500 had been spent on 'Parliamentary expenses'. The latter figure, the report stated, included the hire of Committee rooms, and 'canvassing'.

The London & Birmingham's prospectus contained interesting parallels to the final Great Western one. Like the Great Western's, it drew upon the success of the Liverpool & Manchester Railway of 1826 and offered, like that railway, superior 'safety, expedition and economy' to all other modes of conveyance. The 'expedition' referred to a speed of 15 to 20 miles per hour. 'Economy' encompassed passenger fares at less than half of stage-coach fares, and goods traffic at two-thirds of the cost of conveyance by canal. The London & Birmingham proposed a link to the Liverpool & Manchester that would produce a line between 'the two greatest sea-ports in the kingdom'. The market for passengers on the London & Birmingham consisted of 7 million people. The prospectus claimed that the railway would unite the great manufacturing areas of Great Britain, the Midlands, Lancashire and Yorkshire – the absence of Bristol and the South West from this listing is conspicuous. The prospectus projected an income of £600,000 to £700,000 per annum.

LOCAL SUPPORT FOR THE GREAT WESTERN

The company arranged for various local Bristol businessmen to give evidence to the House of Commons Committee in 1834, and they supported the company's evidence that the route would be of advantage to commerce in the city. The financing of the Great Western also showed the strength of local support for the railway, not least the fact that the members of the 1833 Committee showed their confidence in the potential profitability by investing large sums of their own money in it, as shown in Table 11. However, collectively their contributions were not a large proportion of the Great Western's share capital, amounting to only 8 per cent.

These contributions are recorded in the company's Sealed Register of Proprietors, that is the register of shareholders ordered to have the Great Western's seal affixed to it (hence sealed) at the first proprietors' meeting, on 29 October 1835. The original 27 directors of the company (who included all the members of the Bristol Committee) bought between two shares (George Woolley, a jeweller in Bristol) and 259 (Robert Bright). In total they bought 3,106 shares, 1,803 of these being sold to men who styled themselves 'merchant'.

The Acts establishing railway companies set out in close detail the duties of the directors, but did not stipulate a minimum shareholding. As was the case with Acts establishing canals,

Robert Bright	£25,900	**Table 11: Shareholdings of the**
John Cave	£12,800	**early promoters**
Charles Bowles Fripp	£25,400	
George Gibbs	£14,400	
Thomas Guppy	£7,400	
John Harford	£13,900	
William S. Jacques	£12,000	
George Jones	£13,800	
James Lean	£1,000	
Peter Maze	£23,400	
Nicholas Roch	£23,500	
Benjamin Shaw	£5,000	
John Vining	£22,700	
Total	**£201,200**	

directors had to be qualified in the post by holding a certain number of shares. The Avon Navigation Act of 1712 required of directors an estate in land of the yearly value of £100 per annum, or a personal estate of £1,000. The Great Western's directors had to hold £2,000 in shares, although in at least one case only a single share was held in the undertaking. Thus the company's directors, while investing quite heavily, did not constitute a very substantial portion of the £2,500,000 it was ultimately authorised to raise. Overall, the Committee members actually paid £38,700 less for shares than they had contracted to purchase. Similarly, the 24 directors of the Midland Counties Railway contributed only £85,166 to the £800,000 capital of that company in 1836 (11 per cent). Clearly, then, the directors of some early railway companies did not make substantial financial contributions to their companies, although George Hudson told the Committee on the York & North Midland Bill that he was a 'substantial shareholder' in that company.

As has already been pointed out, none of the promoters of the Great Western came to dominate the company in the way Hudson did his, or as Edward Pease and his son Joseph dominated the foundation of the Stockton & Darlington. By the time of the Gauge Commission, in 1846, Hudson could tell the Commissioners that he controlled nearly 1,000 miles of railways. Two years earlier he had told the Select Committee on Railways on 18 March 1844 that he was Chairman of the Leeds & Bradford, the Newcastle & Darlington, the York & North Midland, and the York & Scarborough companies, and was a director of the North Midland, the Manchester & Birmingham, the Derby & Birmingham and the Midland Counties. He was actively engaged in the management of all these companies except the Manchester & Birmingham. A Return to the House of Commons of all individuals spending over £2,000 on railway shares in 1846 showed that such people had spent collectively £121,255,874, of which George Hudson alone had spent £819,835, more than any single individual. This had been spent on eight schemes, in amounts ranging from £2,000 to £200,000. The present-day equivalent of this spending is no less than £48,370,265 – Hudson has justly been dubbed the 'Railway King'. No Great Western figure appears in this 1846 listing.

Brunel bought 80 shares in the undertaking, and George Stephenson 50, in 1835. Despite his not having a large financial stake in the Great Western, the absence of any single substantial shareholder shown in the Return left the way open for Brunel to assume a dominant position in the Great Western. There was no figure equivalent to George Hudson or the Pease family.

Saunders's letterbook brings out his concern over raising enough capital to enable the Great Western's Bill to go before Parliament, concern that had led to the adoption of the ill-fated 'divided route' proposal. Brunel had put this idea to the Board, but it appears to have originated in a discussion he had with Saunders. He wrote in one of his first reports to the Board, on 8 September 1833, shortly before the concerns expressed by Saunders to William Tothill, the Great Western's other Secretary, that:

> '...from the results of all the calculations that have been made, it appears that the number of passengers likely to travel between London and Reading will not only be greater than any other position on the line, but greater than on any line of equal extent in England... The revenue from such a line must be very large, and will be independent of the continuation of the line.'

The path of the company from foundation to 1840 has now been traced, and, as can be seen, the coming of railways brought about a more widespread share ownership than canals had done, and their geographical spread made their enactment more controversial, and something that physically touched upon the lives of a vastly greater number of landowners than had the canals.

4.
PETITIONS FOR GREAT WESTERN COMPANIES

'A very large portion of the inhabitants of this city [Bristol] have invested their money in the undertaking, from a conviction of the public benefits that would arise from it, and in the fullest confidence that the very best means have been adopted to secure the completion of that measure in the manner best calculated to promote their interests and those of the public generally.'

Petition for the Great Western Bill, 20 February 1834

The Parliamentary process for gaining authority to build a railway began with Petitions to the House of Commons, both for and against the proposed Bill. The promoters would set out the merits of their proposal, and Parliament's consideration of the Bill began the day after the presentation of their Petition. Other Petitions would be heard, both for and against the Bill. Many proposals were lost because the Committee on Public Petitions considered that the allegations in a Bill's preamble had not been 'proved'.

In 1834 the Great Western's promoters petitioned Parliament for leave to bring in a Bill to enable them to establish a line from London to Reading and Bath to Bristol, the 'divided route' as described earlier. This Bill was defeated in the House of Lords, then the following Session (1835) a further Bill was brought forward for the whole route. The petitioning for the various Great Western companies may reasonably be assumed to be a good illustration of a process going on all over Great Britain in the 1830s.

PETITIONS RELATING TO THE GREAT WESTERN INCORPORATION BILLS

Parliamentary consideration of a Bill for a railway always began with the presentation of a Petition, praying for leave to bring in a Bill. When leave was granted, the Bill was presented, usually on the next day the House of Commons was sitting. In their Petition the promoters set out the merits of the proposed railway, and over the rest of that Session Petitions were received by Parliament in favour of and against such a Bill, which were then referred to the Committee on the Bill. In the absence of such Petitions, Bills were referred to the Committee on Unopposed Bills, and usually went through their stages on the floors of both Houses purely formally, that is with no debate. The promoters' Petition for the Great Western Bill was presented to Parliament on 20 February 1834.

The scale of petitioning demonstrates that the 1834 Great Western Bill was both strongly supported and opposed. Twenty-three Petitions were deposited in support, and 51 against.

Seventeen in favour came from towns along the proposed route: Bath, Bridgewater, Cheltenham, Cirencester, Henley, Melksham, Neath, Reading, Shepton Mallet, Stroud, Swansea, Taunton, Tiverton, Trowbridge, Wells and Glastonbury, Westbury, and Wotton-under-Edge.

The scale of Bristol's support for the Great Western can be gauged from the fact that Bristol Corporation's Petition in favour of the later 1835 Bill had 10,550 signatures, collected in only three days; unfortunately, no similar figure appears to be available for the 1834 Petition. Nevertheless, the number of signatories in 1835 suggests a strong degree of support for the Great Western in Bristol, coupled with indignation at the fate of the earlier Bill, which had been fomented partly by the Great Western itself in a leaflet it had issued deprecating the loss of the Bill, which had not been lost 'upon its merits'. Those in support that did not emanate from Civic Corporations were from Bristol: the Chamber of Commerce, the Merchant Venturers, and the Bristol Dock Company.

The 51 Petitions against were of a different character. Twenty-five came from named individuals, including the Earl of Cadogan, who spoke against the Bill in the House of Lords. Other opposition included the Thames Commissioners and the Commissioners of several bridges who would lose income when the railway opened; the Earl of Jersey also spoke in the House of Lords against the Bill, and petitioned the Commons. The proprietors of several canals petitioned, including those of the Kennet & Avon and the Bath & Bristol, and the Commissioners of the Metropolis Roads north of the Thames were also active, as were the counties of Berkshire, Wiltshire and Buckingham. There were also Petitions against from private companies, the Chelsea Waterworks and Bristol Waterworks.

No other railway excited anything like this degree of support or opposition. The Liverpool & Manchester proposal of 1826 had seven Petitions in its favour in the Commons, and 18 against. The Manchester & Leeds Railway, whose Bill was passed in 1836, had 25 Petitions in its favour and 12 against. The North Midland Railway, another 1836 Bill, had 15 Petitions in its favour and 12 against. The earlier North Union Act, of 1834, had six Petitions in its favour and three against. Therefore it is evident that the conflict between public and 'private interests' posed by the development of railways was more sharply focused by the Great Western's legislation than by any other contemporary Bill. This was because of the importance of the two cities linked by the Great Western, and because the railway passed through a heavily populated part of the country.

Lord Granville Somerset (1792-1848) led for the Great Western on the floor of the House of Commons. He had been Member for Monmouthshire since 1818, becoming Lord of the Treasury, Chairman of the Lunacy Commission, and a Privy Councillor. Lord Somerset concluded that

'...this undertaking has, from the commencement, had the misfortune to meet with as great a contrariety of opposition as, perhaps, the promoters of a great public work ever had to contend with.'

The subsequent defeat of the 1834 Bill showed that Parliamentary procedure was still, despite the magnitude of the Great Western Bill, able to provide a telling forum for the expression of interests.

Given the number of Petitions from towns and the fact that they have not survived in the House of Lords, it is of wider relevance that the Petition of the inhabitants of Dursley of 1835 is preserved in Gloucester Record Office. This Petition observes the benefit that would be drawn from any measures that would 'facilitate' communication between large cities in Great

Britain. Dursley could 'look with confidence to the advantages' it would derive from having the Great Western. The railway would diminish the cost and duration of a journey between that district and the Metropolis, and generate 'much greater facilities for the carriage of passengers and merchandise than any now in existence'. The speed and economy of travelling that would follow would stimulate commerce and therefore be to the 'manifest advantage' of the community.

PETITIONS RELATING TO GREAT WESTERN COMPANIES' BILLS

A useful context for the Great Western incorporation Petitions is provided by the petitioning relating to several of the future absorbed companies. All these lines were engineered by Brunel, whose visionary zeal left little room for the day-to-day practicalities of building them within the estimated costs. His companies were not alone in this, however. Despite the scrutiny of the Examiners of Public Petitions, the 1839 Select Committee on Railways reported that it had established

> '...that in almost every case into which they have inquired, the Parliamentary Estimates of the expense of constructing the railways have fallen far short of the actual expenditure... They believe that it may be attributed to the parties promoting the various Bills, as well as the engineers, being devoid of that experience which would have enabled them to form an accurate calculation as to the extent and nature of the work required, the materials to be used, the quantity of land necessary for the purposes of the railroad, and the buildings indispensable for the accommodation of the public.'

Additionally, the Committee referred to the 'over-sanguine expectations and the natural desire on the part of the promoters of the work to keep as low as possible the calculations of the anticipated expenditure, and thus to show their undertaking in a favourable light.' The Committee went on to point out that the cost of land required had frequently exceeded the value estimated before the passing of a Bill.

The Bristol & Exeter Railway
The Bristol & Exeter Railway Company gained the Royal Assent to its Incorporation Bill on 19 May 1836. It was partly financed from the outset by the Great Western, and was leased to it from 1840, becoming fully absorbed in 1876. The line was engineered by Brunel, its Secretary was Charles Saunders, and its locomotives were supplied by the Great Western from the outset. The line opened on 1 May 1844, and the accompanying illustration shows *Actaeon*, a member of the 'Firefly' Class, which hauled the first train. Driven on that day by its designer, Daniel Gooch, it had been built by Nasmyth, Gaskell & Co of Manchester in December 1841, and was ultimately withdrawn in March 1868.

The Petitions relating to the Bristol & Exeter Bill in 1836 are characteristic of the reaction to railway Bills in the 1830s. The relevant records at the Public Record Office contain the texts of half of the 20 Petitions against the Bill, but not those in favour. The Journal of the House of Commons of 1836 records 18 Petitions in favour as well as the 20 against. Like the Great Western, the Bristol & Exeter received Petitions in favour from places along the line of the route: Bridgwater, Sidmouth, Weston-super-Mare, Bristol, Taunton, Exeter, Crediton,

The Bristol & Exeter Act of 19 May 1836.

***Actaeon**, the engine that pulled the first train on the Bristol & Exeter Railway on 1 May 1844. GWR Museum, Swindon*

Dartmouth, Cullompton, Penzance, Plymouth, Devonport, Stonehouse, Bath, Wellington, Bradford and Truro.

Amongst the opposition was the Petition of the Dean and Chapter of Exeter Cathedral, who petitioned as owners of land through which the railway was proposed to pass. They said that they would not 'offer any opposition to the making a railway shown to be required for the public', and asked to be assured that the line chosen was the best 'in regard to the particular benefit of the property through which it may pass'. They further complained that no survey had been made showing the justification for the route selected, and indeed a survey undertaken by the Petitioners had shown a superior line for the railway through Stoke Canon. This would have meant more accommodation for the occupiers and inhabitants and 'much less of injury to the property of your Petitioners than the line proposed'.

Some individuals petitioned against the Bristol & Exeter Bill because the proposed railway would have divided their lands. For example, Ralph Barnes's lands would be crossed by the railway on an embankment for half a mile and he claimed that he had received no notice of 'any intention to make the railway until after the plans had been deposited with the Clerk of the Peace'. He objected that he was 'wholly uninformed' about the survey by Brunel. Charles Saunders captured the spirit of this difficulty in one of his cartoons, implying that the problem of divided land affected even Queen Victoria.

The Rev Henry Creswell had a parsonage and glebe of about 10 acres of 'excellent land, partly ornamental, walled gardens', which would be drastically affected by the railway. He had already been put to 'most serious and considerable expense' by the Bridgewater & Taunton Canal. Creswell was 'unfortunate and harassed' as his premises were again marked out for destruction. More particularly, 'upon well-grounded facts he had every reason to know that the intended line is straight through the front of the Vicarage House, and destroying the same.'

Other petitioners complained likewise about their land being dismembered by the proposed line, including the Petitions of Samuel Ellis and H. H. Mavell, and George Milman, who owned a farm and lands at Bedminster across the homestead of which the Bristol & Exeter company proposed to set its route:

'...close to the house and cutting a trench across the said homestead seven feet deep, by which the said farmhouse will be cut off from the land and both land and house rendered almost useless, and a grievous wrong will be done thereby.'

These Petitions illustrate the juxtaposition of private interest and public benefit that was symptomatic of the development of railways in the 1830s, and was an important theme in the establishment of the Great Western and the companies it came to absorb.

Creswell was also concerned about the powers Parliament was granting to railway companies. He pointed out

'...most plainly and distinctly but at the same time in the most respectful manner to your Honourable House the very great and dangerous power that will be delegated to the above railway company if this oversight in passing the Bill ... be permitted ... to give [to the railway company] a full and unlimited power to pull down and utterly demolish whom they list, but at the same time there has been no clause whatever for rebuilding or putting in place again.'

Creswell therefore sought a clause in the Bristol & Exeter Bill to build a new parsonage. Ultimately, clause 9 of the Bill simply gave the company power to take the vicarage, but imposed no requirement to substitute a new building: 'public good' had triumphed over 'private interests'. The accompanying cartoon by Charles Saunders illustrates that the matter of 'public good' was most acutely questioned by cases in which a railway divided somebody's land, a point of contention much raised in Petitions to Parliament against proposed railways.

The State played the part of defender of the 'public good', and the coming of the railways, because of the magnitude and number of the new undertakings, focused this in a way that previous public works – turnpikes and canals – had not. On the other hand, the Great Western Railway Company experienced opposition from 'private interests' of great significance, notably Eton College and Oxford University, whose importance was such that they had easy access to the floors of both Houses of Parliament to have their interests defended. The railway was one of the longest of the principal companies of the period under consideration: at 117

'The Queen's Staghounds' Narrow Escape on the Great Western Railway. The hunting party has ventured on the line, throwing the hunters into disarray. One unfortunate horse has been decapitated under the wheels of a carriage.' One of Charles Saunders's pen and ink sketches c1840 depicting a hunt disrupted by a train, a satirical comment on the railways' autocratic attitude to those whose land the line ran through. *National Railway Museum, York*

miles it was exceeded only by the Eastern Counties, and therefore acutely focused the question of 'public good' – a railway between the then two premier cities in the land – over-riding 'private interests' – those of private, usually small, landowners whose properties were required in order to effect that 'public good'.

The Great Western was the most expansionist of the early railway companies, by the construction of new lines and by the lease or purchase of a number of others, each of which had to be subject to Act of Parliament. This was a new phenomenon in the British political scene – companies with extensive lists of proprietors or shareholders, and being promoted by a far wider range of people than canals had been. Proprietors were not, as they had been with the Warwickshire Navigation (1723) or the Kennet & Avon Canal (1794), limited to one share each. As we have already seen, the Great Western Railway was launched with 25,000 shares at £100 each, which were sold to 1,443 people, and by 1846 it had issued 253,205 shares, with a total value of £8,160,000.

The Cheltenham & Great Western Union Railway

Evidence of the petitioning for and against the Cheltenham & Great Western Union Railway Bill confirms the foregoing analysis of the Bristol & Exeter. The Cheltenham Railway received its Royal Assent on 21 June 1836 and was opened between 1841 and 1847, partly financed by the Great Western. On 10 February 1836 two named individuals' Petitions were presented against the Bill, and one of opposition from the Thames & Severn Canal Navigation. Landowners in Cheltenham petitioned against the Bill on 21 March and several other individuals the following day.

On 11 April landowners in Gloucester petitioned against the Bill, seeking a re-examination of a proposal for a line from Cheltenham by way of Oxford. On 20 August several more Petitions against from named individuals were presented. To meet one of the objections referred to above, Clause 108 of the Bill imposed penalties on the Bristol & Exeter company should the Thames & Severn Canal be obstructed during the railway's construction. A Petition of inhabitants and owners of property in Gloucester prayed that

> '...the Bill may be re-committed for the purpose of examining the direct line from Cheltenham by way of Oxford. and so much of the said Bill as authorised making the said railway from Cheltenham to Stroud, Cheltenham, Burford, Oxford, Hereford, Northleach, Tewkesbury, and Burford, Ross and Ledbury.'

The Oxford & Great Western Union Railway

The profile of Petitions to the Oxford & Great Western Union Railway Bill is also of interest. Six against came from named individuals, while, most unusually, five Petitions in opposition came from towns along the route, although two in

The Cheltenham & Great Western Union Railway's seal and Act of Parliament.

support were received from the most substantial towns, Oxford and Reading. However, that from Oxford did not originate from the City Council. A feature of the Oxford & Great Western Bill was that, unlike virtually every railway scheme, it was not supported by the city or town it was intended to serve. On 16 May 1838 the Mayor, Aldermen and Burgesses of the City, assembled in Common Council, decided to oppose the Bill, and submitted a Petition to Parliament against it. However, nobody appeared in support of the Petition when it was considered by the House of Commons.

A detailed examination of the witnesses before the Committee on the Oxford & Great Western Union Bill is also of significance. The Bill came before the Commons in 1837, to achieve the link between the Great Western main line and Oxford that had been projected to investors in the Great Western's prospectuses as a great potential object of expansion for the railway. The Commons Committee heard evidence from 47 witnesses, 17 of whom gave evidence against the Bill. The opposition witnesses included three landowners, two farmers, a hotel proprietor, a solicitor, and two engineers (Vignoles and William Moorsom). Surprisingly, the opposition witnesses also included two tradesmen (an ironmonger and a brewer). As just mentioned, and equally eccentrically given the widespread support of towns throughout the country for railways, Thomas Roberson (sic), the Town Clerk of Oxford, appeared as a witness against the Bill.

A profile of those giving evidence in Parliament on railway Bills can be drawn from the records of the Oxford & Great Western Union Railway Company in the Public Record Office. As with petitioning, there is a strong representation from local civic and trade groups. Thus after the evidence of the line's engineer, Brunel, the first evidence came from William Butler, Oxford's Mayor, opposing the Bill. Then followed various Oxford traders and businessmen, including George Davenport, an estate agent, Samuel Bruce, an agriculturist and land valuer from Eynsham, John Edwards, an Oxford ironmonger, and others including a wharfinger, a grocer, a bookseller, and a paper-maker.

To counteract this opposition, expert views were provided, in addition to Brunel's evidence, by William Hemming, the company's Secretary. His evidence concerned the Oxford & Great Western's proposed capital and the company's traffic projections. As Secretary, just as in the Great Western Committee's case with Saunders, Hemming was asked about completely different aspects of the company's promotion than had been asked of the Engineer, although the latter's evidence usually strayed into the Secretary's area. The Oxford Railway's experience therefore exemplifies the range of interests in the development of railways on a local stage, and as with almost all railways, including the Great Western itself, the company's evidence was provided by its Engineer and Secretary, rather than a Board member.

5.
THE PARLIAMENTARY DEBATES ON THE GREAT WESTERN BILLS, 1834 AND 1835

'One and only one pretext against the Bill seemed to have any force as a reasonable ground of objection. It was urged that the line was incomplete as a Great Western Railway between London and Bristol, and that the attempt to secure two portions thereof at first, might subsequently impede a direct Railway communication with the West of England, to which more extensive object, as a measure of admitted national utility, the Legislature could never refuse its sanction.'

Letter to shareholders, 2 September 1834

PARLIAMENTARY PROCEDURES

To be able to open a railway, the promoters had to get authority through a Private Bill in Parliament. This was the incorporation Bill, creating the new railway company with corporate powers. Such Bills gave compulsory purchase powers, and set various conditions on the operation of the proposed railway, including its capital-raising powers. An appreciation of the procedure for Private Bills in Parliament is therefore necessary for any study of the interaction of Parliament and railways in the 1830s.

Parliament's consideration of such Bills began with the presentation of the promoters' Petition to the House of Commons for leave to bring in a Bill. The next day the Bill was brought in and had a first reading, which was purely a formality. Subject to certain financial guarantees, to be discussed below, the Bill then came before the House for a second reading. If successful, the Bill would then pass into Committee, which functioned like a modern-day Select Committee rather than a Standing Committee: witnesses were heard both for and against the Bill, and the Committee reported to the House whether it considered the allegations in the preamble to the Bill had been proved or not.

If they had been, the Bill then went through consideration on the floor of the House, which gave Members the opportunity to table Amendments to specific parts of the Bill (the report stage). The Bill then went through a third reading debate. If passed by the House of Commons, the Bill then went to the House of Lords for an identical consideration, with the exception of the presentation of the promoters' Petition. After a successful third reading in the House of Lords, the Bill under discussion received the Royal Assent, and became an Act.

Timothy Hayter's painting reproduced here captures the Chamber of the House of Commons before it was destroyed by fire in 1834, and this was the Chamber in which the 1834 Great Western Bill was considered. The picture demonstrates the still medieval atmosphere of

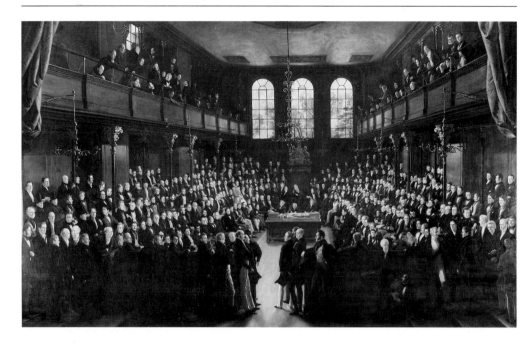

The House of Commons in 1833, by Sir Timothy Hayter. *National Portrait Gallery, London*

the House – British society was changing only slowly under the pressure of industrialisation coupled with political reform, and railways played an important part in accelerating this process.

THE 1834 GREAT WESTERN BILL IN PARLIAMENT

The 1834 Bill was for a railway from London to Reading and from Bath to Bristol, and it came to the House of Commons for its second reading on 10 March 1834, when it was passed by 182 votes to 92. The Committee stage took 57 days. On four separate occasions the House passed Motions giving the Committee power to 'enlarge' the time for its consideration of the Bill. On the third reading in the Commons the House debated, and defeated, an Amendment to the third reading motion proposing that the Bill should be read a third time subject to the Great Western being obliged to apply to Parliament for power to build the railway from Reading to Bath before any construction work could begin. The Bill did not receive its third reading until 23 July.

It then passed to the House of Lords, where it was defeated on its second reading on 25 July by 47 votes to 30. Less than three months after the defeat of 'God's Wonderful Railway', the Houses of Parliament were burned to the ground.

Lord Wharncliffe (1776-1845) led for the Great Western in the Lords. He was to chair the Lords Committee on the Great Western Bill in 1835, picking up false statements circulated by the Bill's opponents. Brunel's viaduct at Hanwell, which is illustrated here, was completed in 1837 and named after Wharncliffe. Under his influence the Lords made an Order requiring the directors of any company seeking to extend its powers to secure the agreement of at least three-fifths of the proprietors, this taking effect in 1846, shortly after his death.

The fate of the 1834 Bill demonstrates the effects of Parliament on the promoters of railway

Wharncliffe Viaduct, Hanwell, with an inset showing Brunel's signature on the original contract for the structure. *GWR Museum, Swindon*

Bills in the 1830s. Concerns about raising sufficient capital for the entire line in time for the Bill's second reading had led to the proposal of the 'divided route', and Robert Palmer (1793-1872), Member of Parliament for Berkshire from 1825, who described himself in Dod's *Parliamentary Companion* as a 'moderate Reformer', leading for the opposition during the debate the following year, began immediately with a summary of what had led to the defeat of the Bill in 1834:

> 'It was not known to Hon Members generally what the Bill before the House really was, for it appeared in the Votes of the House as the second reading of the Great Western Railway Bill, but it was not the case of a railway from London to Bristol, but a Bill of a very different nature.'

He went on to say that the full subscription list of people pledging to buy shares had not been attained, causing the original plan to be abandoned, and that a second advertisement had had to be published for a railway between London and Reading, Bristol and Bath. Palmer concluded that:

Portrait of Robert Palmer by Eden Upton Eddis. *Berkshire Record Office*

'He had stated a strong case to induce the House to reject the Bill. It appeared that the measure was incomplete even as to the plan, and he feared that very considerable injury would be done to the places through which the railway would be carried unless the line was completed.'

The first of many assertions that the Great Western would accomplish the full line came from Charles Russell, Member of Parliament for Reading, and subsequently Chairman of the Great Western from 1839 to 1855, who said that

'...from the observations made, it might be inferred that no *bona fide* intention was entertained to complete the railway. That such could not be the case was simply proved by the fact that the proposition emanated not from Reading nor from any place on the road, but from Bristol itself.'

Reference was also made to the fact that

'...the great outcry which was made for the separation of the countries [England and Ireland] would be stopped by evincing the desire to give every benefit to Ireland that could reasonably be afforded her. If they desired to retain it as an integral part of the Empire, they could not take a more effectual way than by opening the communication a rail-road would give.'

After its long Committee stage, the Great Western Bill returned to the floor of the House for its report or consideration stage, and much attention was then given to the numbers of landowners and occupiers on the line who did and did not assent to the passage of the railway. Parliamentary procedure, in the days before Parliament was overwhelmed by the 'Railway Mania' of the 1840s, was adequate to permit a full and telling expression of views by affected landowners.

Richard Wyvan, Member for Denbighshire, claimed that most landowners over the entire route supported the Great Western. He broke down the assents and dissents between different parts of the route:

'...between London and Reading, those of that class who dissented are only 108, as opposed to 350. Between Bath and Bristol, the proportion is still more decided, 32 only dissenting, while 792 owners and lessees assent.'

The destruction of the Houses of Parliament in 1834 by fire means that official records of the 1834 Committee do not survive, but the Great Western company published a summary account of the proceedings, which was distributed to shareholders. The first evidence contained in this reprint was given by Charles Ludlow Walker, Bristol's Mayor. He told the Committee that he was in trade, sending large brass products to London, of 150 to 200 tons. He described the process of the Corporation's involvement in the foundation of the Great Western, including how he had chaired the Bristol Committee set up to consider the desirability of the proposal. He observed that the climate of opinion in Bristol was 'decidedly' in favour of the line, and that there were 'very few objections'. The line would be 'decidedly advantageous to the commerce of Bristol'.

Walker gave the Committee evidence of the advantages the railway would bring his business, which was typical of all railway incorporation proposals. He had been sending goods to London by water, but had been 'inconvenienced' by delay. The Committee then heard evidence from Sir William Reed, a land agent. He lived near the Liverpool & Manchester Railway, and observed that that railway had led to at least a trebling of the traffic in passengers between Liverpool and Manchester. He told of the practical benefits accruing to agriculture from railways, talking of the 'facility for the conveyance of manure and produce'. The value of land had had 'a very great increase' since the line had opened.

The Committee took evidence from two farmers and various local tradesmen and merchants, including a Bristol sugar-refiner and tea-dealer who referred to the difficulties he had encountered sending his goods from Bristol to London by the Kennet & Avon Canal: he had been 'very frequently inconvenienced by delay'. As an alternative he had tried sending goods by land, but had found that an expensive mode because of 'the danger and delay'. Pilferage was also a problem.

After hearing evidence from James Shepherd, a grocer in Bath, the Committee heard from Thomas Vesey, a tallow chandler and soap-maker from near Bath. The difficulties of communication were emphasised by Samuel Provis, who had been running the second largest carrying company between Bristol and London. Other witnesses appeared before the Committee to confirm this evidence about poor communications.

Lastly, the Company reprint summarised the evidence of Brunel. He was to spend a considerable number of days in the witness box, and emphasised that he had sought, in laying out the line, to do as little damage as possible to 'ornamental property', on instruction from the company, which had resulted in increased costs in some instances.

The Committee went on to question Brunel closely on the line's proposed inclines. The cuttings were favourable, and the deepest was only about 40 feet. The cost of creating cuttings would be about £40 a yard. Brunel discussed how he had formulated his estimate of cost. He had allowed a 25 per cent margin for 'unexpected work', but it had been 'an easy line to survey, compared to other lines in the country'.

Brunel then read various papers to the Committee, including an abstract of his estimate, broken down into geographical sections. His estimate for the section to Reading was typical of that required of any surveyor or engineer by Parliamentary Committees, covering excavations and embankments, masonry, tunnelling, fencing, a London viaduct, locomotive power, and depots in London and Reading. The total costs between London and Reading would be some £666,800.

Brunel then turned to give similar evidence for the Bath to Bristol section, the cost of which he estimated at £960,760. This was followed by a discussion with the Committee about the suitability of Temple Meads as the Bristol terminus. This section of the summary is missing from the copy held by the Railway Museum in Swindon.

Next, the summary covers the evidence to the 1834 Committee of George Stephenson. He had compared Brunel's London to Reading line with the Windsor line and preferred the former, which was 'extremely favourable' with regard to cuttings, embankments and inclinations. Brunel's plan was more favourable than those for most railways. No engineer, Stephenson said, could look at both lines and fail to see the superiority of Brunel's. The line to Reading was particularly favourable in not interfering with 'ornamental property'. Brunel's estimates of cost, Stephenson said, were realistic; indeed, they were 'very liberal indeed'.

Next, the Company report summarised the evidence of Daniel Mosley, a land valuer who had worked for the Great Western valuing land between Reading and Maidenhead with a view to its compulsory purchase under the powers of the company's incorporation legislation. He confirmed the Great Western's evidence as to the adequacy of the sums Brunel had allowed for the purchase of land. He gave the Committee figures for his valuation of the land between Reading and Maidenhead, adding an additional sum for damages sustained by the parties. The Committee, suspiciously, asked him if he had fixed the same value as he would have done had he been an umpire, and he replied that he had 'fixed the full outside value'. Another land surveyor, William Townsend of Bristol, had valued land for the Great Western from Bristol to Twerton, a distance of some 10 miles. He explained his method: he had valued the 87 acres needed at £13,807, to which he had added £4,205 for the cost of buildings.

It is unsurprising that the evidence the Great Western reprinted was so predominantly in favour of the railway; it did not reprint any of the evidence against its proposal at all. In general terms railways were favourable to commerce and communication – all people potentially benefited from them. Their usage would be more widespread, among a wider social range, than was the case with stage-coaches. In specific terms, the level of traffic by stage-coaches promised a very good traffic for the Great Western.

The length of time the Bill had spent in Committee in the Commons ultimately led to its defeat in the Lords at the second reading on 25 July 1834, although, as has been seen, it had obtained its second reading in the Commons by 182 votes to 92. The longest railway thus far incorporated, the Eastern Counties Railway, spent only two days in Committee in the House of Commons, 29 April and 12 May 1836, and one day in the House of Lords, 23 June. The Bill for the Newcastle & Carlisle Railway spent 15 days in Committee in the Commons, and the Committee heard 18 witnesses in opposition, including Robert Stephenson, who also appeared for the promoters of the Great Western in that company's Parliamentary Committee. In 1835 the Great Western Bill would spend less time in Committee than in 1834, although a substantial number of witnesses were heard – 53. Brunel appeared for only one day, as did Saunders. 'Expert' advice was provided by Dionysius Lardner and by Michael Faraday.

Lardner (1791-1859) was a fellow of the Royal Society and professor of astronomy at University College, London. He edited the *Edinburgh Cabinet Library* from 1830 to 1844, and lectured in the United States and Cuba from 1840 to 1845. He settled in Paris where he wrote works on railway economy and natural philosophy. Michael Faraday (1791-1867) was a natural philosopher. He had been an apprentice to Sir Humphry Davy and had travelled widely as his amanuensis. He wrote a major work on the discovery of and properties of chlorine, discovered magneto-electricity in 1831, and made various discoveries about the property of electricity. He was honoured by the gift of a house by Queen Victoria at Hampton Court.

The second reading in the House of Lords, on 25 July, was almost at the end of the Parliamentary Session. The debate began with the presentation of petitions against the Bill, from the Commissioners of the Metropolis Turnpike Roads, landowners in Berkshire, the proprietors of the Kennet & Avon Canal, the Bath and Bristol Waterworks and the Grand Junction Canal, and landowners in Berkshire, Wiltshire, Buckinghamshire, Chippenham and Cheltenham.

Lord Cadogan led for the opposition:

'Because in the first place ... it is an incomplete measure. There is an immense difference between what the high-sounding title of the Bill professes to accomplish, and what its provisions actually purport to do... The railroad, according to the Bill itself, is to extend only from London to Reading; from that place goods are to be transported by the Kennet & Avon Canal to Bath; and they are to be conveyed the remaining twelve miles from Bath to Bristol by another railway. I appeal to your

Lordships whether it is right that the legislature should sanction a measure, the very enactments of which show that it is inefficient for the purposes it is intended to accomplish.'

This he considered a fraud on the subscribers, who had bought shares in the expectation of a complete railway from London to Bristol. However, Lord Cadogan was not an uninterested party to the progress of the Bill. Lord Wharncliffe led for the Great Western, and asked Cadogan if

'...he would give his assent to the road going through his estate [in Middlesex]. If he will ... the plans will be carried into execution. But, he says, "No, you shall not pass through my estate." Then, surely, he has no right to come here and make it a ground of objection to this Bill "that the terminus has been altered"... The fact is ... that communications were held by the parties promoting this Bill with the noble Earl; and everybody must, on reading the report, be satisfied that the understanding between the parties was not that the Noble Earl intended to give his support to this Bill, but that he would give it his consideration, at all events, and not oppose it, since it was no longer going through his estate.'

Lord Cadogan replied that he had indeed seen a deputation from the promoters, and had agreed to withdraw his opposition in return for their offer 'to relinquish their intention of coming through my property'. The effect, he said, had been

'...to disarm him from opposition [as a private individual], but as a public man ... I take it as an insult rather than anything else... My vote shall be decided upon this as upon all other cases, by the balance of good that will be derived to the public in comparison with the interest of individuals.'

Lord Wharncliffe was accused by Lord Kenyon of 'imputing improper conduct to the noble Earl [Cadogan]'. Lord Cadogan admitted that he had appeared before the Committee on the Bill after the terminus had been altered to take account of his objections but that this had not been sufficient to enable him to alter his objections.

Wharncliffe's contribution to the debate was followed by the Duke of Cumberland, brother of King William IV. Cumberland was described by a contemporary as 'a master of narrow-mindedness, selfishness, truckling, blustering, and duplicity, with no object but self, his own ease, and the satisfaction of his own fancies and prejudice.' Any Bill that has not completed all its stages in both the Commons and Lords by the end of the Parliamentary Session is completely lost, and Cumberland drew attention to this major obstacle to the Bill's progress, the lateness of the time:

'...a Committee of the House of Commons sat for so many weeks upon this Bill. I am sure it would be utterly impossible for a Committee of this House [of Lords] to terminate their labours before the end of the Session, if your lordships were to consent to refer the Bill to a Committee at all.'

However, Lord Ellenborough (Joint Chief Clerk of the Pleas for the King's Bench) suggested that

'…if these parties have been disputing for 57 days before a Committee of the House of Commons, one would hope that they had very nearly got to the end of their dispute. If that be not the case, I believe both parties must be extremely unreasonable, and that no length of time will enable them to come to a right conclusion.'

On the argument that the railway might not be completed, he said he could

'…not imagine that the persons, who have subscribed their money to this undertaking, and especially those residing in Bristol, would have done so unless they felt confident that they would ultimately succeed in the formation of the whole line.'

Next spoke the 3rd Earl of Radnor (1779-1869). He was a Whig, and a friend of William Cobden. He actively supported social issues, and introduced to the debate the argument that to go into Committee would put the parties to a 'great and unnecessary expense'. It would be a 'very ungracious' thing for the Lords not to vote out the Bill on the second reading. After all, he said, it was 'about the wildest scheme' he had ever heard of in his life. He went on that the greatest objection was that the Bill was not for a 'Great Western Railroad' at all. While it purported to be a railway from London to Bristol, in reality it was 'quite a different thing'. The Bill was then defeated by 47 votes to 30, and Lord Wharncliffe warned that the message to opponents of Bills to delay progress by any means was a dangerous one.

THE 1835 GREAT WESTERN BILL IN PARLIAMENT

The defeat of the 1834 Great Western Bill caused consternation amongst the investors, and induced the Great Western to adopt new stratagems to secure the passage of the 1835 Act, principally the employment of Osborne Ward, the Bristol solicitors, to promote the Bill, and the abandonment of the 'divided route' that, as we have seen, was a major factor in the defeat. The role of Osborne Ward is considered in Chapter 7.

In 1835 the Great Western Bill therefore came before Parliament with a very different purpose, proposing making the railway over the entire route from Bristol to London. It passed the House of Lords on its second reading by 46 votes to 31, having received its second reading in the Commons by 160 votes to zero. There was no division in the House of Lords on the third reading in 1835.

The Select Committee on the Great Western Bill in 1835 was chaired by Charles Russell, the Member of Parliament for Reading, who was later to become Chairman of the Great Western from 1839 to 1855, before committing suicide in 1856. It was not unusual for someone so closely involved in a scheme for a railway to chair its Parliamentary Committee. Thus the proposal for the Oxford & Great Western Union Railway, which was initially defeated in 1837, was chaired by Lord Harcourt, Chairman of the company and one of the two County Members for Oxfordshire. The 1846 Select Committee on Railways would later recommend an end to this practice whereby Members of Parliament could sit on Select Committees for railways in which they or their constituency had an interest.

The Great Western's main witness was Brunel, who first gave evidence on 24 March 1835. He began by explaining why he had initially considered two routes for the Great Western, south and north of the Marlborough Downs, and told the Committee that he had found the northern one 'superior on every account'. The Committee then explored with Brunel the amount of cuttings he proposed to make, and the effect the consequently larger numbers of bridges would have on the time for the line's construction. However, he told the Committee that the quantity of cuttings was 'comparatively small' compared to lines of similar extent. The result of his surveys was a requirement of 9,750,000 cubic yards of cutting in 127 miles. This was projected by the Great Western's directors as a noteworthy feature of Brunel's engineering, and certainly testified to the quality of his work. The Southampton line's requirement was 15,000,000 cubic yards, the London & Birmingham (112 miles) 13,000,000. This was a testament both to Brunel's skill as a civil engineer and the easier ground over which the Great Western was to pass.

Among the topics of greatest interest to Parliamentary Select Committees on railway Bills during the 1830s were cases in which lines competed with each other. In 1835 a competitor with the Great Western was the Basing & Bath line, which was ultimately to become the London & South Western by merging with the London & Southampton on 4 June 1839, remaining the Great Western's fiercest rival. Brunel told the Committee that the Great Western line was evidently superior to that of the Basing & Bath, and that the opposing line 'would not open any communication between the south of England and the Midland Counties'. The Committee then asked Saunders for a comparative table of the populations along the two lines, and Saunders provided them with population figures within 10 miles of both routes. The total population along the Great Western lines, but excluding London and Bristol, was 96,304 in 16 parishes. The population of Bristol itself in the 1831 Census was 59,074, but the city was growing and by the 1841 Census was 32.8 per cent larger, at 78,450. The Basing & Bath, according to Saunders, would serve a population of 62,892 in nine parishes. Along a proposed branch to Gloucester, the Basing & Bath had an almost identical level of population in six parishes. Thus the Great Western was affecting a far greater number of different landowners over its distance than the Basing & Bath.

The Committee then subjected Brunel to a detailed examination on his estimate of the costs of construction, which, he told them, was £2,190,820, to which he had added a larger sum than usual of about 10 per cent for contingencies, bringing the cost of the Great Western up to the level of capital it sought, £2,500,000 (see Table 9). This sum compared to that originally projected to the Bristol Committee by Brunel in 1833 of £2,805,300. Only 3% of the 1835 estimate was for locomotive power and carriages.

A further example of Parliament seeking to protect 'private interests' was the clause in the Great Western Act barring the company from crossing roads on a level, and therefore obliging it to erect bridges. Here, again, is an example of the quality of Brunel's civil engineering: he told the 1835 Committee that he had included bridges from 12 to 30 feet wide for roads over the railway, of which there were 'very few', whereas on the railway between London and Southampton there were 'a great number'.

It is of significance to observe from whom Parliamentary Committees took evidence on private legislation concerning railways. Foremost among the witnesses, of course, were the promoters of the Bill. In the Great Western's case, this meant Isambard Kingdom Brunel. The two chairmen of the Great Western between 1834 and 1840, Benjamin Shaw and William Unwin Sims, made no appearances before Committees, despite the Great Western putting forward seven Bills during the period to 1840, two of which did not receive the Royal Assent.

This absence was not unusual: George Carr Glyn also made no appearances at Westminster for the London & Birmingham, of which he was Chairman. By contrast, George Hudson did not leave this important task to his engineers: during his career he appeared 76 times before Select Committees, usually on his own Bills, although he also appeared before the Great Western Committee in 1835. The absence of Brunel's chairmen emphasised his importance as the most publicly visible officer of the Great Western. Company Secretaries, like

Engineers, were favourite witnesses. Saunders appeared three times for the Great Western, including both incorporation Bills, in the period to 1840, and 79 times during his whole career, up to 1863. Likewise the Secretary of the Midland Counties Railway, John Fox Bell, appeared for the Midland Counties in 1836. An exception to this absence by most chairmen was the 1839 Select Committee on Railways, a massive review of public policy towards the developing railways. This took evidence from the chairmen of ten different railway companies, including – for the Great Western – William Unwin Sims, the Great Western's second Chairman, after Benjamin Shaw.

Committees were always unsure how to obtain reliable expert advice that was independent. Nowadays Select Committees appoint specialist advisers, but the solution in the 1830s was to summon nominally independent experts. Foremost among these were two strong advocates of the 'narrow' gauge, Sir John Hawkshaw and Nicholas Wood. These two men had come to assume a position of considerable influence in the development of early railways, and were regarded as luminaries on railway matters. Wood (1795-1865) was a colliery owner at Killingworth in Northumberland, and a close associate of the Stephensons. He wrote a gospel for the development of railways, *A Practical Treatise on Railroads*, in 1825.

Wood was not, however, a dispassionate judge between the gauges: a Parliamentary Return of 1846 showed that he then held £48,480 in two 'narrow' gauge railways, the Liverpool, Manchester & Newcastle-upon-Tyne Junction and the North Gravesend. That sum equates to over £2.5 million at today's prices.

Sir John Hawkshaw (1811-91) was, like Wood, a keen advocate of the 'narrow' gauge and on no fewer than 486 occasions gave evidence to Parliamentary Select Committees on private Bills relating to railways. Their advocacy of the 'narrow' gauge made them implacable enemies of Brunel, and neither bought any shares in the Great Western, although George Stephenson did spend £3,000 on the company's shares, and Wood bought 150 shares in the North Midland Railway, a Stephenson-engineered line promoted by George Hudson, authorised on 4 July 1836. The esteem in which they were held can be reckoned by the fact that when the Great Western's Liverpool proprietors forced the Board to reconsider the use of the broad gauge, the Board turned to Hawkshaw and Wood to run experiments of the relative advantages of the two gauges. Such a proceeding was not unprecedented: James Walker and John Rastrick had been summoned to assess the merits of two routes George Stephenson had proposed for the line of the Liverpool & Manchester. Rastrick (1780-1856) had built an iron bridge at Chepstow in 1815, and engineered the Stratford & Moreton Railway in 1823. He was a judge at the Rainhill Trials, and became the first railway engineer to be elected a fellow of the Royal Society, in 1837.

It is not surprising, given the weight accorded to these men's views by, particularly, the Great Western's Liverpool proprietors, that Brunel hated them with a passion. Brunel's arguments against Wood and Hawkshaw's observations are collected in the British Library, together with both gentlemen's reports. Their experiments favoured the 'narrow' gauge, although Brunel wrote to his Board arguing that some of Sir John Hawkshaw's measuring instruments had been faulty. The depth of Brunel's devotion to the Great Western and his fury at the report of Wood and Hawkshaw is shown by the fact that two days after Christmas, on 27 December 1838, he reported to the Board his reactions to the pair's report. He told his Board that the task of refuting the report would be 'an easy and comparatively agreeable task'.

Evidence that George Stephenson did not have the same crusading zeal that Brunel had for his broad gauge can be seen in the fact that he appeared only 15 times before Select Committees during his career, including that of the Great Western in 1834. The colossal number of Sir John Hawkshaw's appearances before Select Committees on railway Bills means therefore that the dominance of the 'narrow' gauge might arguably be more appropriately attributed to Hawkshaw than to Stephenson.

The Great Western Select Committee, as Select Committees on railway Bills commonly did, took a close interest in the extent of local support for the railway, and the local status of the civic bodies supporting it. Public meetings took place at Bridgwater, Bristol, Cheltenham, Cirencester, Devonport, Exeter, Falmouth, Gloucester, London, Plymouth, Stroud, Taunton, Truro, and a number of other locations in Cornwall, most of which Tothill, the Great Western's Bristol Secretary, attended.

The Select Committee then turned to the geographical origin of the subscriptions. Tothill told them that the subscriptions had come 'chiefly' from towns 'immediately interested' in the Great Western. He did not tell the Committee, if he was aware of it, of the significance of the Liverpool subscriptions, which were to number 1,127 shares in the Sealed Register of proprietors (5 per cent of all shares, the third largest number sold in a single location after Bristol and London, and the largest source of shares not on the line of the railway). The Committee discussed with Tothill the opposition of the Basing & Bath Railway. In September 1834 Tothill had written to that company to propose some independent consideration of the merits of the two proposed lines, and its Secretary had replied that his directors could perceive 'no benefit' from any such review: 'the Act of Parliament has determined the line of the company, and it can now only proceed upon that line'. Tothill told the Parliamentary Committee that the reasons for this had been the Basing & Bath's 'inferiority in point of execution and construction and especially in point of revenue'.

The Committee then took evidence from Charles Saunders, and closely questioned him on the Great Western's estimates of the likely traffic in passengers and goods on the proposed line. He provided a table of likely traffic returns, but it is among pages missing from the manuscript held by the House of Lords Record Office. However, the evidence of the Great Western to the 1834 Committee had contained similar estimates.

Saunders told the Committee that subscriptions had continued to come in after the defeat of 1834: thus in Reading three-quarters of the subscriptions came in after the defeat. Clearly the people of Reading still had great faith in the proposed railway. Saunders was asked about the different places that had subscribed, but not about Liverpool subscribers. According to Saunders, 'a great many' of the landowners along the route – at least 20 per cent – had subscribed. The Committee pressed the point, asking how extensive the subscription of the Corporation of Bristol was: Saunders put it at 100 shares.

The Reading *Chronicle* was not happy at the passage of the Great Western Bill in 1835, and reported on 5 September 1835 that the Royal Assent had been given. Despite the level of local support for the railway, the newspaper observed that

> '...we have not yet heard what decision will be made by the inhabitants of the towns on the high road between Reading and Bristol, but we should advise them to prepare for the great change which the railway will effect in their trade.'

Railway development thus had a major impact on the functioning of Parliament and its development in the aftermath of the Reform Bill of 1832. Parliament was intrigued by the emergence of companies established to generate 'public good' through private profits, and there is consequently much evidence of contemporary reaction to the development of railways in the records of Parliamentary Select Committees.

6.

CONFLICTS AND PROCEDURES: WHO SHOULD ESTABLISH BRITAIN'S RAILWAYS?

Why no State controls? It was 'very much from the practical difficulty of dealing with the great number of railway Bills that were brought before Parliament in the years 1836 and 1837, and the very protracted and difficult nature of the inquiries; and it was felt that to have undertaken that sort of supervision, at that period, when so little was known about the principles which were to guide railway legislation, might have converted the Board of Trade, in fact, into a tribunal for doing nothing else than attending to Railway Bills pending during the Session.'

W. S. Laing, head of the Railways Department, Board of Trade

Awholly new phenomenon in Britain consequent on the development of railways was the question of the provision of public services by private companies. The expansion of the Great Western and other companies raised the ogre of monopoly, and this was of some concern to Parliament, despite the State's reluctance to assume any type of proactive role with regard to the development of railways. This chapter assesses the debate, then gives detailed consideration to the expression of the problem in the pamphlets of William Galt, an expression well-regarded enough by contemporaries in Parliament for him to be called, as has been seen above, to give evidence on his views to Gladstone's 1844 Select Committee on Railways, from which sprang the first elements of public control of railways.

The problem was summarised by the 1839 Select Committee on Railways in its Second Report:

'...it does not appear to have been the intention of Parliament to give to a railway company the complete monopoly of the means of communication on their line of road; on the contrary, provision was made in all or most of the Acts of Incorporation to enable other persons to place and run engines and carriages on the road, upon payment of certain tolls to the company.'

The Committee then went on to state that such an aim on Parliament's part was idealistic, but it was clearly insufficient to merely allow any person to run his own engine over a track, since support for that operation, such as water, had to be provided.

The Committee expressed concern at the difficulties that arose from 'an extended intercommunication throughout the country, solely maintained by companies as acting for their private interests, unchecked by competition and uncontrolled by authority'. Over their routes, railway companies had no competition: their arrival quickly brought canal companies to their knees, and stage-coaches suffered from being slower and unable to carry substantial quantities of passengers or goods.

The unknown author of *The Environs of Reading* wrote in 1840 that

'...few save the pedestrian can properly appreciate the important addition to a road constituted by the rapid and ever-changing traffic of stage-coaches and omnibuses. We must not, however, descant too fondly upon the subject, as it is probable that within a few months the completion of our very fine line of railway will totally annihilate the agreeable variety and the hanging woods of Englefield and Beenham will no longer echo back the nocturnal challenge of the mail-guard's horn.'

The assessment of the 1839 Committee's report that public utility and private profit were not necessarily contradictory brought up a problem that has dominated British political life since that time:

'...it will be found to be the opinion of some of the witnesses that the interests of the railway companies and of the public can never be at variance.'

The question of whether railway companies should simply provide track, or also engines, carriages and coaches, caused some disagreement among the witnesses. The practice of some railway companies, such as the Liverpool & Manchester, had always been to act as the exclusive carrier on their lines. A different policy was followed by the Grand Junction Railway, the London & Birmingham, and the Great Western itself. The 1839 Committee considered the conflict between the needs of the public and those of the proprietors and recorded two views: first, that the country had benefited from railways, a view that was beyond dispute; and second, that it could not be assumed that the interests of the public and those of the proprietors would always overlap.

Extensive controlling blocks of power in the 1830s were focused on two men, George Hudson, who had substantial financial interests in a large number of companies, and Brunel, who had engineered all the railways on the broad gauge, which comprised one-third of the country's railway mileage by 1846, although, as has been seen, he was not a significant shareholder in any of the companies he engineered.

Amalgamations that were taking place were not creating a monopoly. The principal example was that in 1846-7 of the Grand Junction, the London & Birmingham and the Manchester & Birmingham to form the London & North Western Railway. Professor Simmons has called this an 'end-on' amalgamation, not creating a monopoly. The monopolistic tendencies in the North of England were focused on George Hudson, who said in evidence to the Gauge Commissioners in 1845 that he controlled more than 1,000 miles of railways. The Great Western had 1,443 proprietors in 1835, the largest of whom, a gentleman from Denmark Hill, held 775 of the 22,911 shares. The directors of the company were not substantial proprietors, and 21.16 per cent of the proprietors held only one share each. The company was not therefore dominated by any single financial interest. George Hudson did, however, establish a monopoly for himself: at his height in 1849 he had financial control of the railways of Northumberland, Durham, North and East Yorkshire, Nottinghamshire and Leicestershire, most of Derbyshire, and the Eastern Counties.

Certainly the State was no match for Hudson in extent of control. The Duke of Wellington decried the lax way in which the State had failed to control the development of railways in the United Kingdom, referring in Parliament in 1838 to the

> '...improvident manner in which the Legislature had passed the railway Bills without any guard against their monopoly and mismanagement.'

Professor Simmons comments (1986) that 'the Government shrank from that duty and introduced no measure at all'. The 1839 Committee blamed the lack of control over railways upon Parliament rather than the Government:

> '...the Legislature having practically given to those companies a complete control over all the great channels of intercourse throughout the country, your Committee deem it to be indispensable both for the safety and convenience of passengers and the public to prohibit so far as locomotive power is concerned the rivalry of competing parties on the same line, although such prohibition involves the continuance of the monopoly... A supervising authority should be exercised over all the arrangements in which the public are interested. It would seem advisable that this control should be placed in the hands of the Executive Government, and it might be expedient to vest it in a Board to be annexed to the Board of Trade.'

Ultimately, the Railways Department of the Board of Trade was established in 1840. The horror with which the Board's officials viewed the taking on of the task of monitoring the activities of railway promotion is set out in the evidence of Samuel Laing, head of the Railways Department. The Committee recommended that 'no new railroads should be opened for the conveyance of passengers until an inspection had been made under the sanction of the Board of Trade'. The Committee was well aware of how great a change in the position of the State it was proposing, and was therefore not prepared to recommend that this controlling authority over railway companies should be established until

> '...the subject shall have undergone consideration and discussion... Your Committee do not hesitate to repeat their opinion that some such superintending Board will be required for the purpose of protecting the weak against the strong, counteracting the evils consequent upon monopoly.'

As the railway revolution of the 1830s matured, debate followed as people became aware of the workings of the monopolies outlined above. This debate was focused by solicitor William Galt (1809-94) in a pamphlet he wrote in 1844 castigating the 'profiteering' occurring on Britain's railways. The issue of whether the State should establish a Government-controlled 'system' of railways, as existed elsewhere in Europe, was the subject of several pamphlets. Galt's conclusions furnish an important example of the old world coming into conflict with the new, and illustrate a new exposition of the role of the State.

He argued that the 'evils and abuses' of railways were inherent in them, and resulted in excessive charges for carriage:

> '...entrusting the railway monopoly to companies who neither have nor profess to have any object in view but their own gain, is in the highest degree injurious to the best interests of the nation.'

	2nd class fare	Cost to company	Cost per 100 miles
GWR	28s 6d	10s 10d	6s 7d
L&BR	22s 6d	7s 5d	7s 8d

Table 12: Great Western and London & Birmingham fares compared

Galt was, however, gloomy about the prospect of any reduction in fares coming voluntarily from the railway companies themselves: he said that there was no prospect of a reduction in fares without the interference of the Legislature, because it was not in the interests of the railway proprietors, who drew greater profits from high fares. To make his point, Galt cited evidence of the fares of the Great Western and the London & Birmingham, as shown in Table 12.

He went on to observe that fares differed fivefold between different railway companies. He did not attribute these to genuine differences in costs: they arose because high fares suited 'the interests of the proprietors'. The roots of Gladstone's reforms in 1845 to introduce trains costing a penny a mile, and thereby open up the benefits of the new system of rail travel to all classes of society, can be seen in Galt's pamphlet.

Galt's figures comparing the Great Western and London & Birmingham bring out a consequence of the former company pursuing Brunel's visions of a quality railway. Galt wrote that 'the present scale of fares ... is as high as totally to prevent some classes from travelling'. His views are an interesting illustration of an attitude towards the operation of capital that was to lead to an increasingly interventionist Government.

Galt's pamphlet concluded that there was no justification for these discrepancies, and that 'the whole system from beginning to end is artificial and arbitrary'. The public was being 'taxed without representation' in one of life's great necessities. In fact, the range in fares on the largest railways was not as great as Galt claimed. In 1842 the average 1st Class fare per mile for the 11 largest British railway companies was 2.5d per mile, ranging from 3.5d on the London & Brighton down to 2.33d per mile on the South Eastern. The figure for the Great Western was 3.03d per mile. Great Western fares were therefore 21 per cent higher than the average. In 1838 the 1st Class fares on the Great Western were, according to evidence given to the 1839 Select Committee on Railways, three times greater than on 'open' carriages.

Galt's pamphlet is nevertheless of importance in illustrating the effect of the financing of railways on the political consciousness of the nation. Attention was being given to the proper role of the State, and contrasts were being observed between practices in this country and abroad. Galt was sufficiently highly regarded to be called to give evidence to Gladstone's 1844 Select Committee on Railways, from which sprang the Act of 1844.

The Great Western's 1834 and 1835 Bills are important examples of the practical effects of railways on constitutional development in Great Britain. The phrases 'private interests' and 'public good' were being bandied about during the Committee stages on both Bills, but had been absent from the Parliamentary consideration of canal legislation in the early 18th century.

The 1844 Select Committee on Railways also drew attention to the 'enormous disproportion' in the costs of building railways in this country and abroad. As already mentioned in Chapter 2, the Committee quoted the Belgian Minister of Works, who observed that the lower cost of Belgian railways could not be attributed to the lines crossing an easier geography. Neither, the Committee observed, could the difference in expense be attributed to superior efficiency. The Committee then analysed the causes of these extra expenses. Land

and compensation were approximately double what they cost in Belgium, while Parliamentary expenses, which averaged £700 per mile over the whole of Great Britain, did not arise in Belgium at all. In addition, law charges averaged £1,000 a mile more in this country than in Belgium.

A further distinction between foreign and British railroads was pointed out to the 1839 Committee on Railways by Robert Stephenson, who pointed out that there was no tax on railroads in Belgium and France. In the six months to 30 June 1841 the Great Western paid £15,940 in Government duty for mileage and £3,161 in rates and taxes. Receipts in the same period were £212,947, and the company was still making a gross loss.

The Committee then went on to set out the cost of construction of British railways, and found that these had varied between about £9,000 per mile (the Dundee & Arbroath) and £59,800 per mile (the Manchester & Leeds). The range is truly staggering, and accounts for Galt's views. The Great Western was cited as the third most expensive, at £56,300 per mile; the London & Birmingham cost £53,100.

Thus these monopolistic railway companies raised the issue of whether railway development should be left to 'private interests' for it to be most effectively promoted. There was no contemporary tradition of State control of the means of communication – the Post Office was not to be introduced until 1840. The 1839 Select Committee on Railways discussed the desirability of a national system for railways with Joseph Baxendale, Deputy Chairman of the South Eastern Railway, who had spent 20 years working for the 'great carrying company', Pickford. He told the Committee that a customer who wanted goods conveyed to a particular city would have to wait until the railway company had sufficient demand to that location to fill a wagon. Rather than simply take his goods to the railway, he would send them with a carrier who traded specifically with particular locations. He was asked if the public would be better accommodated if a person could take his goods to the railway's warehouse for onward transmission, but he did not believe that companies could become carriers beyond their own lines. He was asked if he thought 'that the companies belonging to those lines that join your line would make some general arrangement to receive your goods and forward them along their lines in the same way as they receive passengers?' Baxendale thought there would be difficulties. He could not, however, explain the problem without the Committee going with him to a warehouse.

The 1844 Committee attempted to bring some general controls to that development, and Parliament's system for handling it. Thus the First Report proposed that all future legislation should contain a clause stating that an Act to establish a company could not exempt that company from the provisions of any general Act relating to railways. The Sixth Report of the Select Committee on Railways accordingly proposed that the length of Bills could be reduced by a general Railways Bill. This was an effort to control the size of railway legislation, which has already been remarked upon. The effect of the Committee's findings was almost immediate: the Act to establish the Berks & Hants in 1845 was 51 clauses long, and that to establish the Birmingham & Oxford Junction in the same year ran to 83 clauses, so the logical outcome was the promotion of the Clauses Consolidation Act in 1845, which removed the need for many clauses in railway Bills which were of general application.

An overview of the effects of the quantity of railway Bills on Parliament was provided by the Third Report of the Select Committee on Private Bills in 1847. This dealt with two principal points: how Parliament could cope at a practical level with the numbers of Private Bills, and how the expenses for promoters and opponents might be controlled and reduced. Erskine May, Clerk of the House of Commons and one of the Examiners of Petitions for Private Bills, described the procedures his Department had established in order to ensure that Petitions were dealt with in sequence of deposit. He had introduced different procedures for Opposed and Unopposed Petitions, and thereby had virtually eliminated the delay in their hearing. The Committee recommended that advertisements of the intention to apply to Parliament should be published in local newspapers as well as the *London Gazette*, and that the current practice of fixing notices to church doors was no longer adequate.

As has already been remarked, a further cause of delay was that all Bills went through Parliament from the House of Commons; the result was an excess of business at the beginning of the Session for the Commons and at the end for the Lords. The Committee accordingly recommended that Bills should be commenced in the House of Lords as well as the House of Commons. An additional complication was the number of Committees sitting simultaneously on Private Bills, and the 1847 Committee on Private Bills therefore recommended that they should be grouped by a Committee of Selection. To accelerate the consideration of Private Business, the Committee recommended that Petitions should be first sent to the proper Department or Board, which would report thereon to the House. These Inspectors would be 'directed to inquire first as to whether the provisions and conditions of the public General Acts … had been complied with by the petitioners'. The Committee sought to assess the average number of railway Bills each Session, and their cost. It based its account on the years 1842 and 1843, the average number in these two Sessions being 161.

Despite the profitability of railways to their proprietors, there was a clear perception in Britain that railways constituted a public benefit. In the 18th century the only substantial developments of the arteries of communication had been the development of canals and turnpikes. The emergence of railways in the 1830s and subsequently was a dramatic escalation of this process, and the boost railways gave to communications – principally newspapers – meant that the sense of a 'public' need that should over-ride 'private interests' was beginning to emerge. This development is evidenced in the proceedings of Private Bill Committees on railways, which paid close attention to the public benefits that would be derived from proposed railways. Samuel Laing, head of the Railways Department of the Board of Trade, gave extensive evidence to the 1844 Select Committee on Railways, although in that capacity he did not give evidence to Select Committees on individual companies' proposed Bills. His evidence offers a retrospective view of the practical consequences for civil servants and the Government of the development of railways in the 1830s.

THE USE OF PARLIAMENT BY GREAT WESTERN COMPANIES

The important development in the working of Parliament taking place at this time under the pressure of railway legislation can be illustrated by an analysis of the numbers of the Bills/Acts brought forward during the entire history of the Great Western and the companies merged with it before and at the Grouping, and the extent of their use of the Parliamentary process. By 1840 15 different companies that were ultimately to form part of the Great Western had been established, and during that period they had put forward a total of 47 legislative proposals. Prior to nationalisation the 249 companies that were to form the post-1923 Great Western group had put forward 2,061 legislative proposals (of all Great Britain's major railway companies, the Great Western alone retained its identity after the 1923 Grouping, and the accompanying cartoon of November 1922 shows that Brunel's arrogance was still a dominant theme of the Great Western in the 20th century, just as it had been a major characteristic of the company in the 1830s).

The conflict over the 1834 Bill had shown the tension between public and private interests, which was to lead to demands for railway reform, chiefly by taking railways under public ownership. The Great Western particularly illustrated this conflict, because of the length of the line and hence the extent to which its enactment presumed the compulsory purchase of private lands. Professor Simmons has observed that 'it was an immense undertaking to build a railway over a hundred miles long. There was no precedent for such an achievement anywhere.' This tension resulted ultimately in Gladstone's 1844 Railways Act.

The seriousness of the task of dealing with the volume of Petitions was alluded to by Erskine May, who told the 1847 Committee that there had been in the previous Session (1846) no fewer than 487 Petitions for Private Bills, of which only 13 were withdrawn before going before the Examiners. May described how Opposed Petitions were dealt with after Unopposed Bills, as they took longer. A 'very laborious' part of the proceedings was the comparison of the number of subscriptions and the estimate, yet despite the volume of business his Department had always succeeded in making its reports to the House within 24 hours of hearings being concluded.

One practical consequence for Parliament of the promotion of railways was that it was common for railway companies' directors to be Members of Parliament. Two Great Western examples already mentioned were Robert Palmer, Member for Reading, and Charles Russell, Reading's second Member of Parliament and ultimately Chairman of the company. This led to concern over how impartial such Members would be if they found themselves sitting on the Select Committee examining an incorporation Bill. The 1844 Select Committee on Railways was to recommend that Members of Parliament who could be regarded as 'locally interested' in the outcome of a piece of railway legislation should not sit on the Select Committee on that Bill. The course of Great Western legislation showed how acute this problem could be: the 1835 Committee on the Bill was chaired by Charles Russell, who was soon afterwards to become Chairman. Similarly, the Committee on the Liverpool & Manchester in 1825 had been chaired by General Gascoigne, Member for Liverpool.

THE 1839 SELECT COMMITTEE ON RAILWAYS

The debate over public control was sharply focused by the Select Committee on Railways in its Second Report of 1839. During the period under consideration, when all the principal railways in the United Kingdom were established, Parliament came under heavy pressure, to an extent not previously experienced, and the concept of public control of undertakings established for the benefit of the public in addition to their proprietors took root. The result was a major Select Committee inquiry into the development of the railways – the Select Committee on Railways – which reported on 26 April 1839. The length of the inquiry evidences the extent to which Parliament was coming to question the 'laissez-faire' policy of public control of the development of railways that had hitherto held sway. The Committee asked 5,991 questions of 45 witnesses, including Robert Stephenson and, for the Great Western, Charles Saunders.

The significance of the inquiry is shown by the number of railway company chairmen who appeared before it, including those of the London & Croydon, Greenwich, Eastern Counties, South Eastern, Northern & Eastern, Grand Junction, Newcastle-upon-Tyne & Carlisle, Leeds & Selby, and Stockton & Darlington.

The inquiry reflected the scale that railway legislation had assumed. Thus the Great Western Act of 1835 had 250 clauses, in 1836 the Bristol & Exeter's had 160, the Cheltenham &

Great Western Union's 131, and the York & North Midland's 230. Railway Acts were longer than canal Acts, such as that for the Kennet & Avon Canal in 1794, and were also much more numerous.

The 1839 Committee considered at length the question of public good against private interest, which had been so strong an undercurrent of the failure of the Great Western Bill of 1834: the Committee described 'the immediate interests of enterprising individuals and the convenience and intercourse of the whole community' as a subject of much importance. The Committee set out the extent to which this new problem of public advantage had been provoked by the development of railways: they said that the rapidity of the growth of railways coupled with the large amounts of capital involved gave the Committee 'a strong disinclination' to interfere.

The Committee was also horrified by the advent of share dealings promoted by the development of the large share market in railway stocks:

> '...your Committee also call the attention of the House to the manner in which the shares ... are made the subject of speculation, the insecurity and inconvenience of the course of dealing, and the evasion practised upon the Revenue.'

Concern was additionally expressed in the report at the need to ensure that companies obtained the subscriptions from those who had taken out a contract to purchase shares. The Eastern Counties Railway's Secretary told the Committee that his company had determined to sue defaulting proprietors, but Saunders told the Committee that no Great Western shares had had to be forfeited. The forfeit of shares for this reason was not unusual: the Bristol & Exeter was authorised to issue 15,000 £100 shares, and 4,127 of them had been forfeited on account of arrears upon the calls. The total loss to the company, after making allowance for those sold to other proprietors for the benefit of the company, was £117,611 2s 6d.

The Committee then turned to the question of railway companies acquiring monopolistic powers, as described above, not in the sense that they swept aside the competition of canals, but that the companies themselves were assuming control of the carriage of goods and passengers over their lines, rather than simply providing motive power for other companies to use. The Committee observed that to give people the right to have their wagons and carriages on trains did not of itself obviate the monopoly danger, as railway companies still had to provide stations.

The Committee gave credit to railways for the standards of safety achieved:

> '...it may be confidently stated that very few accidents occasioning any serious injury to passengers have occurred... It does not appear that the velocity of conveyance is necessarily attended with that degree of risk which many persons unacquainted with this new method of travelling had anticipated.'

The Committee was therefore 'unwilling' to put forward proposals that might restrict the successful operation of speculations that had been of such benefit to the country. It observed that Parliament had given the companies 'complete control' of their lines, and should therefore only act with a view to public safety.

However, the Committee concluded that the establishment of some 'supervising authority' would protect 'the general liberty of the subject':

Concerns about the growth of monopolies centred on railway companies assuming control of the carriage of goods and passengers over their lines, rather than simply providing motive power for other companies to use. This J. C. Bourne drawing shows a Great Western livestock train near Bath.

Courtesy of Bristol County Record Office

'...it is clear that the general interests of the community must sometimes be at variance with the interests of railway proprietors, and that in such cases the combination of capitalists, held together by common advantage and guided by able directors, will probably prevail against the disunited efforts and casual resistance of the public.'

This supervisory authority was to be vested in a Board under the control of the Board of Trade, whose officials were horrified at the thought that they might be instructed by Parliament or by the President of the Board of Trade to take on the task of monitoring the activities of railway promotion. However, the Committee ignored these reservations and recommended that no railway should open for the conveyance of passengers without having been inspected and approved by the Board of Trade.

Underlying the whole debate was the question of whether public control would lead to a more productive use of public capital than the expression of free enterprise, and whether the best development of the railway system would come if a public board were established to regulate development, as had happened in Belgium.

7.
THE GREAT WESTERN'S SUCCESS, 1835

'To our charge for time occupied in the details of the arrangements in preparing to apply to Parliament for the whole line. Almost daily attendances in communication with the directors and the secretary. £5,727.'

Osborne Ward account, 11 August 1835

THE ROLE OF OSBORNE WARD IN THE INCORPORATION OF THE GREAT WESTERN RAILWAY, 1835

B runel and the promoters of the Great Western had found that to get a Bill through Parliament was a complicated business, requiring professional assistance. The accounts of the Great Western for 1834 make no mention of using solicitors, Parliamentary Counsel, or any specialist help. It is therefore reasonable to assume that, like so much of the early history of the Great Western, legal matters were handled by Brunel. The fate of the 1834 Bill showed that, while an outstanding civil engineer, he was no lawyer.

As a result, the first thing the company did, within days of the defeat of the first Incorporation Bill in 1834, was to appoint a firm of Bristol solicitors, Osborne Ward, to act for it. The firm's successors in Bristol, the national law firm of Osborne Clarke, still hold their predecessors' original accounts to the company, and kindly made them available to the present author. They cover almost every aspect of getting Parliamentary sanction, including negotiations with landowners and lobbying of Members of Parliament. They also cover the preparation and deposit of the plans with the Clerks of the Peace, and visits to particular landowners. The ultimate result of their work was, of course, the success of the Bill in 1835.

It is evidence of the dominance of Brunel that all this enormous amount of work had fallen on his shoulders in 1834. That alone, leaving aside his intolerance of the need to observe the political niceties of cultivating Members of Parliament, is evidence that he was taking too great a load on his shoulders in running every aspect of the Great Western at that time, and the failure of 1834 was the perhaps inevitable consequence. His talents lay elsewhere, certainly not in politics.

The Board, 'it appearing that the appointment of solicitors ... would be an addition necessary, and that it would tend materially to save time and to facilitate the proceedings in the present state', resolved to appoint Osborne Ward as the company's solicitors. The firm took on the bulk of the responsibility for guiding the new Bill through Parliament in 1835, but despite the significance of their role in the company's promotion, MacDermot's justifiably

Mr Jerre Osborne (*left*) and Mr William Winsford Ward.
Reproduced by permission of Osborne Clarke Solicitors

classic history of the Great Western (1927) makes no mention of it. Significantly, the firm's account is for work done from 4 August 1834, only a few days after the 1834 Bill had been defeated in the Lords. This unique document illustrates how the solicitors became actively involved in the promotion of the Bill, an essential role that had, in 1834, been carried out by the activities of particular directors.

The accounts reveal the procedures gone through in the 1830s to secure the passage of a Private Bill through Parliament, and are important not least because no similar account appears to have been found for any other railway company, although some much less detailed correspondence of the Stockton & Darlington's solicitor is referred to below.

Osborne Ward were 'occupied in the details of the arrangements preparing to apply to Parliament for the whole line'. They attended the weekly meetings of the Committee in Parliament, and also public meetings at Bristol, Bath, Chippenham, Cirencester, Cheltenham and Stroud. They negotiated 'with landowners for permission to make surveys', and undertook 'very many attendances on different parties in Bristol, on canvassing for shares and for the general affairs of the company'. They also charged for 'folding, addressing and arranging in districts many hundred letters, prospectuses, pamphlets, and other papers, in preparing and copying lists for canvasses for shares, in analysing the lists of ratepayers in the City, from the Books of the Collector of Rates, and ascertaining and affixing the addresses to the names of such ratepayers, and arranging them in alphabetical order.'

Osborne Ward were also responsible for organising the contribution of directors to the promotion of the company. Their account covered 'very many attendances on the Directors to solicit their personal attendance in London in the canvass of Members of both Houses'. The firm was the most frequent recipient of correspondence from the Great Western: the company's letterbook records Osborne as having been sent 26 letters in the second half of 1834 alone. The extent of the work involved in the promotion of the Bill is further shown by their account for 'general correspondence ... which occupied the time exclusively of one Principal and one Clerk for 33 days'. Their account also shows the scale of work involved in promoting the Bill, including a bill for the time of six Clerks on 'correspondence and other attendances'; this work had occupied no less than 654 days, and the company was charged £1,030 for that item alone.

Osborne and Ward undertook journeys with directors to procure shares and support: their account mentions journeys to Bath, Castle Combe, Falmouth, Liskeard, Penzance, Plymouth, Redruth, Truro and Wells. Osborne billed for 'time spent in travelling for the purpose of explaining to the several landowners the mode in which the line was intended to pass'. The solicitors also prepared the Book of Reference, the list of all properties to be taken and the owners and occupiers, together with a brief description. This involved them 'in establishing the ownership and occupation of property along the line of the proposed railway, and in drawing and examining alphabetical and other lists for the use of the canvassers of the landowners'.

Osborne Ward charged for 'attendance on the principal subscribers in Bristol, to secure their execution of the Deed in time to enable the Secretary to deposit the subscription list in the Private Bill Office, containing subscriptions to the amount of half the capital, as required by the Standing Orders, previous to the Bill being read a second time in the House of Commons.' They also negotiated with particular landowners. Their account includes 'Mr Osborne's journey and attendance on Mr Heywood, Lord Clarendon's steward, at Devizes, with a view to procure a withdrawal of their opposition by the offer of an immediate arrangement of the value and compensation to be paid for their land.' Lord Clarendon had 49 separate units of property in Wiltshire listed in the Book of Reference for the 1835 Act, more than any other individual and including farms, plantations, cottages, gardens and a mill pond. Similarly, the largest numbers of units of properties owned by a single individual to be taken under the London & Birmingham's Act of Incorporation were 51, owned by the Marquis of Hertford in the parish of St Michael, Coventry, and 53 owned by Earl Howe in Duddeston and Birmingham.

Although Osborne Ward's accounts record something of the style of negotiations that the Great Western had with major landowners, they contain no record of any dealings direct with Ministers. However, some hint does survive of such negotiations for the Stockton & Darlington Railway. That company's solicitor, Francis Mewburn, wrote on 22 February 1819 to one of the two chief promoters of that railway, Edward Pease, that he had 'had an interview with the Lord Chancellor... He is too sly an old fox to give his consent... He said he should not give his support ... till he was perfectly acquainted with the [line's] merits ... and he stated a variety of objections which he admitted I had satisfactorily obviated.'

Much humbler property owners were also seen by Osborne Ward, evidence of how exhaustive was their attention to the passage of the Bill. For example, on 8 and 9 May Osborne travelled to see Colonel Magan, who had petitioned Parliament against the Bill, and the firm described him as 'a dissentient landowner who, after an explanation of the mode in which the line affected his property, stated that he was not opposed to the measure, but had dissented under the impression that his property would be very considerably injured thereby.' Similar problems with landowners had been encountered by the promoters of the Stockton & Darlington: with just two notable exceptions, the landed gentry in the county of Durham had opposed the passing of the Act.

Osborne Ward were also engaged in securing the evidence to place before the Committees in Parliament. In May, after the Bill had passed the Committee of the Commons, Osborne billed for 'journeys from Bristol to South Wales, Devonshire and London and attendances during these days in procuring evidence for the Committee of the Lords', which occupied him for 19 days. The solicitors expressed their personal confidence in the prospects of the company by buying shares in it: Osborne bought two £100 shares, and Ward 61. Later, in 1846, Osborne was to spend £27,500 on two railway schemes, the Birmingham, Wolverhampton & Dudley and the Cheltenham & Oxford. The present-day equivalent is over £2.5 million – clearly he had been pleased with railway investment.

The solicitors' attention to detail thus took the promotion of the 1835 Bill to a much more professional level than had been the case in 1834, and landowners were dealt with on an individual basis. The organisation of the appearance of witnesses before the Committee was also made much less random than it had been. Osborne Ward wrote to Messrs New & Birch, solicitors of Newport in Wales, asking them to organise 'evidence of some intelligent person' in favour of the Great Western Bill. They particularly referred to the need for a statement of the 'general extent of the mineral and agricultural produce of South Wales', and the desirability of giving this product access to the London market. New & Birch replied that while they were not subscribers to the Great Western, they were convinced of the favourability of the scheme for the mineral trade of South Wales.

Osborne Ward's account for 1835 came to £5,727, some £340,610 at today's values. They had played several roles of vital importance in the founding of the Great Western: the preparation of the Bill; the enactment of the processes involved in obtaining property needed along the company's route; the setting out of that route; and lastly the amassing of the capital necessary for the company to go before Parliament.

THE GREAT WESTERN'S REACTION TO THE 1834 DEFEAT

Brunel's role in the emergence of the Great Western was of great significance. He appeared 220 times before Select Committees for the Great Western and the companies of which he was the engineer, almost once a month for 25 years. Other engineers did not assume the same familiarity with Select Committees: Robert Stephenson made no appearances at all for the London & Birmingham (which he had engineered) in 1833, while in the same year Joseph Locke made none for the Grand Junction, which he had engineered. George Vignoles appeared just six times before the Select Committee on the Midland Counties Bill in 1836.

The early development of the Great Western was therefore dominated by Isambard Kingdom Brunel. He suggested that the Great Western should lease the Bristol & Exeter Railway, in a report to it of 23 February 1840; this was the largest single railway the Great Western ever acquired. He also suggested to the Board the adoption of the broad gauge. The London and Bristol origins of the company emerged at once, at the first meeting of the promoters, a joint meeting of the Bristol and London Committees. The title 'Great Western' was there adopted (although in the Parliamentary Committee on the Bill one of the opposing Counsel described it as neither 'Great' nor 'Western').

The Great Western's promoters were shocked at the defeat of the 1834 Bill, which had occurred despite the support of George Stephenson at the Select Committee stage. The Great Western company itself and Brunel in particular were enraged by the defeat and produced a publicity sheet that was sent to Members of Parliament in 1835. It drew to their attention the changes that had occurred in the Bill, principally that the route was no longer incomplete. The Great Western said that its Bill

'...is now brought before Parliament in a perfect state. Instead of a Bill for two sections of the line only ... the application to Parliament now embraces an entire line of railway between London and Bristol.'

The directors had told their proprietors that the Bill had passed the House of Commons in 1834

'...after a most searching and protracted investigation, and had been defeated by the House of Lords chiefly upon the question of time, which ... would have been insufficient for another investigation before a Committee of the House of Lords.'

The Commons Committee had sat for 57 days, and the Bill had received its third reading on 23 July. There was therefore no prospect of a similar length of consideration by the House of Lords in the remaining two and a half months of the Session, which included the summer recess. The directors said that

'...the opposition had been maintained against the Bill with unprecedented perseverance... The circumstance evinces at once the importance of the undertaking, and the real merits of the case, which triumphed over every difficulty in the House of Commons, where alone they came under investigation.'

The Great Western company said that the divided line 'was but a partial benefit compared with the whole line, which was in truth the original purpose of the company, and the completion of which they have ever regarded as their sacred duty.'

The proprietors agreed to appeal to Parliament in May 1835 for legislative sanction 'under very different circumstances'. They said that the Bill had been amended 'materially' in response to concerns expressed in 1834 by 'private interests'. Foremost, the railway was complete between London and Bristol. Assenting landowners occupied 92 miles of the route, dissenting 23.25. That was a superior proportion than on the London & Birmingham, which had not been opposed in Parliament, and was still improving as the promoters worked to 'conciliate or satisfy by every reasonable and just concession' the grounds for dissension.

The appeal said that 'a sum exceeding £2,000,000' had been subscribed by people living in 'those parts of the country through or in the direction of which the railway is to be carried'. The promoters described this as 'unparalleled support', half of which had been subscribed since the defeat of 1834. This showed the 'estimation in which this particular measure is held in those Districts most interested in the construction of a Western Railway.'

The appeal concluded that 'the promoters are fully prepared to prove that in point of levels, economy of construction, and the number of important towns and places approached by this railway, a greater degree of public advantage will be effected than by any other line that could be suggested to the West of England.'

The Great Western company had therefore taken account of the expression of views in 1834 made possible by the procedures of Parliament. It claimed that arrangements it had made with landowners meant that whereas in 1834 those dissenting from the Bill had numbered 113, occupying 45 per cent of the land on the line, the position in 1835 was only 20 per cent, and that of the £2,000,000 subscribed, half had been received since the 1834 defeat.

THE GREAT WESTERN RAILWAY ACT 1835

The Great Western Railway Act of 1835, running to 251 clauses, showed what substantial pieces of legislation such Acts were. It began by empowering the proprietors to raise £2,500,000 for the undertaking, in £100 shares. Some other railway companies, such as the London & Birmingham, sought a similar level of capital, and it was not remarked upon by the 1834 or 1835 Parliamentary Select Committees on the Great Western Bills. Thus, although the Great Western was one of the most expensively capitalised companies, this did not of itself attract attention to the Bill in the 1830s. Equally, the £100 value of the shares was not exceptional, even though the present-day equivalent is £5,947. The Cheltenham & Great Western Union, the Taff Vale and the Bristol & Exeter companies were also capitalised at £100 shares. The Great Western's Sealed Register of proprietors of 1835 listed the 1,443 separate proprietors who had subscribed towards the capital, an average shareholding of £1,596 (very nearly 16 shares each), a present-day equivalent of around £94,000.

The Great Western Railway Act, 1835.

The Act then excused the Great Western from 'unintentional' errors preventing it carrying out its works, and set various details governing the construction of the line, including the power to take lands, and penalties for obstructing persons employed in building the Great Western. Powers were given to prevent obstruction during floods of the River Colne – the accompanying Charles Saunders cartoon illustrates the risk to steam locomotives of the Thames flooding!

The Act then turned to deal with landowners. It gave the Great Western power 'to treat' for the purchase of lands, the value of which was to be set by Commissioners, and directed how disputes between the Great Western and certain mortgagees were to be settled; landowners were compelled to deliver a 'statement of their estates and claims' within one month of receiving notice from the Great Western. Sheriffs, jurors and witnesses making 'default' were to be subject to a penalty, and the jurors were to sit under the same regulations

'The Flood on the Thames Junction Railway enveloping an extensive steam engine belonging to the Company', a pen and ink sketch by Charles Saunders, c1840. *National Railway Museum, York*

as the courts at Westminster. If people asked for a jury, they were to enter into bonds 'to prosecute their complaint and to pay expenses'. Three clauses set out the application of differing levels of compensation. The Great Western was empowered to enter lands 'on payment or tender of purchase money'.

The Act then dealt with the Earl of Manvers's land, exempting it from a stipulation of the breadth of land to be taken for the Great Western; regulations were set for drainage upon his lands, and he was empowered to erect a bridge across a street the Great Western was required to form on his estate. The Great Western was to make this under his direction and to repair it. The most significant turnpike road the Great Western was projected to cross was the Bath Road, and regulations were made for lighting the line where it crossed the road. The trustees of the Bath Roads had to consent to any alteration in the levels of their road, and the Great Western was to repair bridges connected with the Bath Roads.

The Act then set out provisions relating to canals. Its manner of crossing the Wilts & Berks Canal was stipulated, and compensation was to be paid for stopping the navigation. The engineer of the canal was to direct the construction of bridges where necessary, as was the engineer of the Grand Junction Canal. If that company was to make a double towing path at Paddington, the Great Western was obliged to allow the same to pass through its bridges, and it was to compensate the Grand Junction if passage of the canal was impeded. The Act set out provisions for Metropolitan roads that were similar to those for the Bath Roads as regards bridges and lighting. The Great Western in London communicated with the London & Birmingham Railway, and the latter's Engineer was to direct the two railways' communication. The Great Western was not to cross the London & Birmingham Railway on a level, nor to interfere with that railway.

Where the Great Western was to intersect 'small parcels' of land, the company was 'compellable' to purchase all the land. Two clauses then governed the land of Messrs Wood, preventing stations or buildings being erected there. Another specific landowner mentioned was Oriel College, Oxford: the company was obliged to purchase its Vicarage House at Twerton. Certain clauses then protected mines, setting out the ownership of mines under the railway, and stating that no shafts were to be sunk under it. The opposition of Eton College resulted in a clause prohibiting the Great Western from making a branch through Eton, building a station within 3 miles of Eton College, and compelling the Great Western to erect a fence on each side of the line near Eton.

The Great Western was required to erect gates for the convenience of landowners beside the railway, and if these were insufficient, the landowners were empowered to erect them at the Great Western's expense. Clause 110 stipulated that the Great Western was to fence the railway through private lands. Two clauses protected the Coombe Lodge estate. The Act then made regulations for the conduct of the Great Western's business: the holding of the first and subsequent General Meetings; the notice to be given of these; the voting at these meetings; the form of proxies; and how they should be cast through the Secretary of the Great Western. The guardians of share-owning lunatics and minors were to vote on their behalf; however, according to the Sealed Register there were no lunatics among the proprietors, and four minors held four shares in total.

Detailed regulations were made for the directors of the Great Western: they were to be chosen at the first General Meeting; they were to serve a fixed term, going out of office in rotation; they could be re-elected when they went out of office by rotation; the General Meeting to choose directors had to be composed of proprietors with a total of at least 2,000 shares; and no Officer of the Great Western was to be a director. Their powers and duties were specified, as were their powers to appoint sub-committees. Any contract signed by three of them was to be binding, and a Book of decisions, proceedings and accounts was to be kept. The Great Western's Chairman or Deputy Chairman had to preside over any meeting of the Board, and the 30 original directors of the company were named.

Provisions were then made for making by-laws, for keeping accounts, the declaration of dividends, and for the issue of share certificates. Provisions were also made for the payment of calls on shares, and proprietors were empowered to sell their shares, but only after all due calls had been paid.

Detailed provisions then followed on the payment for the use of the railway. The Great Western was empowered to provide and charge for locomotive and other propelling power, and to charge for the carriage of passengers, cattle and goods. Controls were set for the carriage of small parcels and for travelling short distances, and rates were 'to be charged equally'. The rates and tolls were to be conspicuously displayed, and in the absence of such display the Great Western's power to charge would lapse. Clause 186 prevented toll collectors 'misbehaving'.

Provisions then followed on the assessment of the proper tolls for owners of carriages and goods wagons, and how differences concerning weight were to be determined. The carriages used on the railway were not necessarily constructed by the Great Western, but the company had to approve them. The same applied to engines. Owners were to put their names on the outside of their carriages and wagons. The railway itself was not to be used as a passage for

Another Saunders cartoon of c1840, 'The gentleman who was locked up because he had lost his ticket'.
National Railway Museum, York

horses or cattle, and owners and occupiers of land adjoining the railway were to pay a toll to cross it. Anybody found walking on the railway was to be subject to a fine. Equally rigorous conditions were imposed for travelling without a ticket, and the accompanying Charles Saunders cartoon captures the essence of this situation! The Act made it illegal to obstruct the railway, and in cases of dispute two Justices of the Peace were to adjudicate. If the Great Western failed to pay compensation for damages, the sum was to be levied by distress of the Great Western's goods. Detailed stipulations were set out for policing the railway, including the appointment and powers of special constables. Anyone aggrieved was enabled to appeal to Quarter Sessions.

Protection was given to the directors, who would not be personally responsible for acts done lawfully for the Great Western. Compensation was to be made to the proprietors of Maidenhead Bridge over the Thames, who would lose the toll income they had been drawing from users. None of the compulsory powers of the Act were to be put in force until the whole of the expense of the undertaking had been subscribed for. The Great Western could sell land it did not ultimately need. Clause 237 empowered the proprietors to raise more money, if necessary, by mortgage, and the Great Western was authorised to increase its capital stock by raising the amount by shares. Detailed provisions were set out for raising further funds by mortgage, but any money raised from the Exchequer Loan Bill Commissioners was to have priority for repayments. If the Great Western paid off a mortgage, it was empowered to borrow the same sum again. All land set out in the Schedule of the Act had to be bought within two years of the Royal Assent, and all the powers of the Act were to lapse if the Great Western was not completed within seven years. If the Great Western was abandoned, the land was to revert to its original owners. The consequent opportunity for objection to be made to Bills on technicalities was great.

8.
COSTS FOR THE PROMOTION
OF RAILWAYS IN THE 1830s

'With respect to the advisability of pursuing such an expense I believe you fully agree with me in my opinion of the importance of perfection in the rails, and I have no hesitation in saying that I am confident that, admitting the full difference of £500 per mile to be an excess in the original outlay, that excess will be amply repaid in the first few years of working in the diminution in the mere cost of repair and maintenance of the Way, while the gain in economy, facility, and perfection of transport would be cheaply purchased at double the cost.'

Brunel's Reports to the Great Western Board, 13 September 1836

Comparisons between the costs of construction of the largest railways have already been made. However, costs had to be incurred before any earthwork could begin. To get Parliamentary sanction was not free and, indeed, the costs of this part of railway promotion, which did not occur elsewhere in Europe, were very much complained of by railway promoters. Additionally, before construction could begin, money had to be spent acquiring the land on which the railway was to be built. The Parliamentary and law charges that the promoters of railways had to meet were a cause of great concern to them, particularly when coupled with the charges they had to pay for land and compensation. The cost of appearing in Parliament to contest railway legislation was significant, and there was much dissatisfaction at the sums companies had to pay to promote their Bills in Parliament. The result of the new, heavy use of Parliament to promote railways in the 1830s was deep dissatisfaction at the cost of obtaining legislation, a dissatisfaction that surfaced in the work of a Select Committee in 1844 and others shortly thereafter.

This problem was not peculiar to the passage of the Great Western Bill: the House of Lords 1846 Select Committee on Railways drew attention to the fact 'that the total amount expended in contests before the Standing Orders Committee ... must be exceedingly large, and it is to be feared that a large proportion of this expenditure has been worse than useless.' The House of Lords Committee cited two examples of such expense: one promoter had had to keep 100 witnesses waiting for three weeks to be heard by the Standing Orders Committee; another had cited a company spending nearly £1,000 a day for ten days waiting to be heard.

The 1847 Select Committee on Private Bills gave figures for the cost of the promotion of Bills in Parliament. The fees paid in 1844 were £40,963 for 159 Bills passed in that Session. In 1844 there were 490 Petitions for Private Bills, and the fees paid up to 30 June were £96,109. The Committee went on to propose a system of local examination of legislative proposals, to save promoters and opponents the cost of coming up to London. Erskine May told the Committee that he could not estimate how much expense had been saved to witnesses by new practices for the hearing of Petitions, since the detention of witnesses in town had been the 'chief expense' for promoters of private Bills.

This question was closely considered by Samuel Laing, secretary to the head of the Railways Department at the Board of Trade, where he prepared Gladstone's Railways Act of 1844. He resigned in 1845, becoming Chairman of the London, Brighton & South Coast Railway from 1848 to 1852, a Member of Parliament discontinuously between 1852 and 1885, and Finance Member of the Government of India from 1860 to 1865. His time at the Board of Trade meant he actively supported the provision of cheap excursion trains on the London, Brighton & South Coast Railway, which was to become exceptionally lucrative. Laing referred to the question of the cost to small landowners of defending their interests in Parliament against railway promoters in his pamphlet on railway taxation, published in 1849.

In this pamphlet he did not question that profitable railway companies should pay high quantities of income tax, newly introduced by Robert Peel, but the current system of financing parishes was clearly iniquitous for railways:

> 'The existing law under which the railway companies are compelled to pay large assessments proceeds on the principle that a railway is essentially improved land and that of the total capital invested in the undertaking, all that cannot be shown to have been invested in strictly moveable property – such as engines and carriages – must be taken to be invested in land.'

Evidently the development of the role of the State taking place at this time presupposed finance for it, and Peel's introduction of income tax was part of this process, and was to contribute substantially to the higher cost of operating a more proactively supervisory role for Government. However, railways exposed the weakness of the then current system of local taxation in the new world of railways, and Laing's views are an important bridge between Government and the railway companies, given his career in both.

The costs for the Great Western of obtaining the sanction of Parliament were set out in the report of the Board to the proprietors for 1835. The company had spent £7,466 on Parliamentary agents' fees, £8,500 on Parliamentary expenses, including witnesses and hire of Committee rooms, and £38,771 on two firms of solicitors (Osborne Ward and Swain, Stephens & Co), which included counsel.

This compares with the cost of getting the Wilts & Berks Canal Bill through Parliament in 1793, which was only £5,797. As we have seen, Osborne Ward alone charged the Great Western £5,727 for their work on the promotion of the 1835 Bill in Parliament. The Board of the Bristol & Exeter was so horrified by the charge of its solicitors, Osborne Ward again, for the promotion of its Bill in Parliament that in 1838 it resolved to ask them to reduce it by 10 per cent. The solicitors replied that they had done their best to keep costs down, but would agree to reduce the bill from £1,751 to £1,600. Thus the costs of the promotion of Bills in Parliament, per mile, ranged from £653 for the Bristol & Exeter to £2,702 for the Liverpool & Manchester, suggesting that Osborne Ward had indeed kept their charges to the former as low as possible.

Land and compensation were significant elements of the cost of launching railways, and generated debate immediately after the 'Railway Mania' of the 1830s that forms the basis of this book. The House of Lords Select Committee on Compensation considered the matter in 1845, and much of its evidence related to experiences during the railway revolution of the 1830s. The

Committee was appointed to examine methods of assessing fairly the value of property to be taken to build railways, and also how to set fair compensation for the injury done to residences.

The main point of consideration was, unsurprisingly, the assessment of a reasonable valuation to be paid for land by railway promoters, and the Committee recommended that in addition to the land value a surplus for severance of 50 per cent should be paid. A great source of contention in the Committee's evidence was whether the assessment of value should be based upon the rental value of a property or its sale value. The latter values were then depressed, so this policy militated in favour of the railway companies. The Committee drew attention to the fact that 'large houses never paid as much in rent, in any case, as the cost of building them'. 'Thus,' the Committee said, 'if a railway takes a house that cost £10,000 to build, they only pay what could be got for it, what it would sell for, together with additional compensation for taking it compulsorily.'

PUBLIC OWNERSHIP OF GREAT BRITAIN'S RAILWAYS?

The discussion of the assessment of charges for land and compensation led to public debate over the issue of public ownership of railways in Great Britain. Although Britain was not taking any steps along the path of public ownership, unlike other European countries, the question was discussed by the 1839 Select Committee on Railways. It drew attention to the difficulty it had had in reaching any conclusion, a difficulty that had

'...arisen from the recent origin of railway communication, from the rapidity of its growth and from the variety of unexpected results consequent upon so great a change in the internal communications of the country.'

The Committee then referred to the 'strong disinclination to interfere hastily with undertakings of such national importance', and was therefore affected by 'great caution' in offering any opinion to the House. The foremost examination of the question of the balance of public good and private interest in relation to railways was to be conducted by the 1844 Select Committee on Railways, under the Chairmanship of William Gladstone. Although post-dating the years covered by this book, much of the evidence on which its findings were based was taken from our period, when so many railway companies were receiving their Acts of incorporation.

It was considered important to encourage the continuing development of railways, which were accepted to be of national importance, while at the same time attempting to control the income the companies were deriving from their operations. Thus the 1844 Select Committee on Railways observed that

'...it is manifestly of great national importance to give countenance and aid to the investment of capital in domestic improvements ... and the Committee doubt whether the establishment of railways in this country does not afford a more remarkable instance than can be cited from any analogous subject matter of immense, certain and almost uniform benefit to the public, combined with a very moderate standard of average remuneration to the projectors.'

The Committee alluded to the need to establish some form of public control of the development of railways: 'In the opinion of the Committee it is desirable to reserve to public authority the means of forming a judgement.'

The expansion of the demand for railways was anticipated by the 1844 Committee: it observed that undertakings were receiving more support from the owners of landed property, and that

'...the improvement of trade and redundance of capital in the country, combined with the prevailing indisposition to run the risks which have rendered some kinds of foreign investment so disastrous, the Committee anticipate a very great extension of the railway system within the next few years.'

Evidence of the scale to which railways transformed the capital markets in the first half of the 19th century can be gauged by the fact that the Kennet & Avon Canal had a capital of £420,000 in 1794 for a route mileage of 86.5, from Reading to Hanham Lock in Bristol. The Lidbrook Railway, a tramway authorised in 1809, had a capital of £35,000 in shares of £10 each. By contrast, several Great Western companies were capitalised at over £700,000, far in excess of former levels of calls for public capital.

Having determined upon a railway from London to Bristol, it was clearly necessary for the Bristol Committee to have a route surveyed and estimates of cost drawn up. Brunel had already been provisionally appointed by it on 7 March 1833, and this was confirmed on 27 August. Having resolved to appoint a highly gifted engineer, and having received from him very technical reports that had persuaded it to adopt the broad gauge as well as to build the line at its two extremities, the Great Western Board nervously wrote to George Stephenson. He replied to their

'...inquiries relative to the line between London and Bristol, in which you particularly refer to the practical construction of the work... I beg to state that I have examined the whole of the important parts of the proposed line, and consider it judiciously selected, not only as regards the execution, but also the working of the line when executed.'

Stephenson was similarly consulted by the Provisional Committee of the Whitby & Pickering Railway about the route proposed by its engineer. As has been seen, the report of the Great Western directors to the proprietors of 29 October 1835 had praised the modest amount of excavations.

The role of the engineer of early railway companies was significant because of the crucial role they played on the Parliamentary scene. In the Great Western's case, this was shown by the fact that of the 57 days the Great Western Bill spent in Committee in 1834, Brunel was in the witness box for 11. However, while the 1835 Committee held 53 evidence sessions, Brunel was in the witness box for only one day, probably because he had been so exposed before the earlier Committee. Saunders appeared for one day, as did William Tothill (secretary of the Bristol & Exeter before becoming Bristol Secretary of the Great Western). Other engineers, while usually leading for their companies in the House of Commons, were not as exposed as Brunel.

Parliamentary Committees were dangerous places for engineers, and the experience of his father may well explain why Robert Stephenson did not appear for the London & Birmingham. Just how perilous the occupation of engineer to a railway company in the 1820s and 1830s was had been shown by the sacking of George Stephenson by the Liverpool & Manchester, after his disastrous performance as a witness in the Commons led to the defeat of that company's Bill in 1825: 'One query after another was answered by "I do not recollect", or "I did, but I do not recollect", or "It may, I cannot speak of it", or "It was a mistake".' The first engineer of the Midland Counties Railway had produced an estimate of the cost of that undertaking that was shown by another engineer, Vignoles, to be wholly inadequate. Vignoles replaced George Rennie as engineer, and the capital of the Midland Counties was increased from £600,000 to £800,000 to finance his improved layout of the line. Another railway engineer, Joseph Locke, who among other railways engineered the Grand Junction, suffered a nervous breakdown as a result of the pressure of early railway promotion.

Brunel did not suffer the fate of Stephenson or Rennie at the hands of his directors, despite his responsibility for the failure of the 1834 Bill, caused by his suggestion of a 'divided route'. Indeed, he was commended in the biography written by his son in 1870 for his patience in dealing with landowners and Members of Parliament.

The Great Western's Bristol Secretary, William Tothill, gave evidence on 23 June 1835. He was not asked questions relating to the engineering of the line, but about the demand for the Great Western and the means by which it had been established. He described the mechanics of the Great Western's inauguration, dealing with the appointment of a Provisional Committee. He made it clear that the Provisional Committee had come to no conclusions as to the route of the railway, but had followed Brunel's advice on the line of the Great Western through Marlborough, selecting

'...the northern one, on account of its superiority in the engineering point of view, having the summit level much less and being much superior in a commercial point of view in as much as it commanded a larger revenue.'

He was asked in greater detail than Brunel on the towns the railway would serve.

Charles Saunders, again unlike Brunel, was asked about the reaction of the directors to the defeat of 1834, and he told the Great Western Select Committee that they 'determined to make application for the whole line, and for that purpose to open a subscription list for an additional number of 15,000 shares, 10,000 having been subscribed for the first Bill.' Tothill was asked about the public meetings the Great Western had held to promote the railway, and the reaction of these to the proposal: the meetings were 'very numerously attended', and 'remarkable for having a very large proportion of the respectable classes' in attendance.

A further critical reaction of the directors to the defeat of 1834, additional to the decision to seek authority for the entire line as outlined above, was the decision to take the legal work of promotion out of Brunel's hands, and to appoint solicitors to act for them; Osborne Ward's role has been considered in Chapter 7.

In conclusion, railways illustrated the modernisation of the State that was taking place during the 1830s, particularly under the influence of Gladstone and Peel. The State was assuming a much more active role in the scrutiny of proposals for railways than had been the case over canals in the previous century, conscious that railways affected a vast number of people, as promoters, landowners and shareholders. Railway incorporation therefore played a critical role in the modernisation of the State, drawing Government forward from a medieval role into one better equipped to deal with the demands of representing the interests of people who were threatened by these large, new corporations, and needed to be protected from them.

9
PRIVATE INTERESTS AND THE GREAT WESTERN

'In a case where a railway goes in front of an old ruin, for instance Jervaulx Abbey or Bolton Abbey, or any other well-known abbey, and goes near it so as to spoil entirely the picturesque effect of the abbey, on what principle do you compute your compensation?

I am not aware of any such case, but I rather think the company would be advised, and that they would consider, that the public utility must prevail, and that they should pay nothing for any loss of beauty, or any thing else... I think that for the mere destruction of an object of beauty or interest, we should not have to pay anything.'

Edward Driver, the Great Western's surveyor,
to the Lords Select Committee on Compensation

E dward Driver, quoted above and one of the Great Western's surveyors in 1834, also advised elsewhere that if a railway ran near such a ruin, the promoters would be advised to build a station near it, to increase the profitability of the line. While, however, he knew of no such instances, the railway revolution did affect different categories of landowners, from the large to those who occupied merely a 'hovel'. In this chapter the assault on private interests is first illustrated by two major institutions, Eton College and Oxford University; both had direct, personal access to the Floors of the Houses of Parliament, which in each case contributed substantially to the defeat of, in the first case, the Great Western Bill of 1834 and, in the second, the Oxford & Great Western Union Bill in 1837, both of which were lost in the House of Lords.

Driver's account of his methods in assessing land values, described below, constitutes an important illustration of a process going on all over Britain during the railway revolution of the 1830s, while examples of different categories of landowners are used to illustrate their reactions to the Great Western: first a major peer, the Earl of Carnarvon, followed by an account of the collective reaction of landowners in Berkshire, and the reactions of two individuals – Colonel Tynte and Sir John Slade – to the Bristol & Exeter Bill, a Great Western client company. All give an interesting insight into the process of railway companies compulsorily purchasing property.

THE ASSAULT ON PRIVATE INTERESTS

All Britain's early major railway companies were incorporated in the 1830s, and their development brought the conflict of public and private interests on to the political scene for the first time, a conflict that has run through British politics ever since. The Great Western's

1835 Bill was remarked upon during the debate in Parliament for the extent to which it represented an assault upon private property. The Great Western's Book of Reference, a document listing all the property a railway was to take under an Act of Parliament, listed 2,359 units of property. During the second reading debate in the House of Commons in 1834, Sir Thomas Freemantle had

'...to complain of the immense extent of the Schedule to the Bill; the lists of the lands, tenements, houses, &c, that were to be forcibly taken from their owners in order to carry into effect this half-measure extended to over 42 pages... Upon reference to the London & Birmingham Railroad Bill, he found that although the line extended to 110 or 120 miles, the Schedule comprised only 19 pages.'

The Eastern Counties Railway, at 126 miles the longest railway authorised at its date of incorporation on 4 July 1836, required 1,350 units of property, 10.71 units per mile compared to the Great Western's 21.41. The London & Birmingham required only 4.17 units of property per mile, in 66 parishes (617 in total), including George Cowley's 'hovel and yard' in Kilsby.

This comparison with the Eastern Counties and the London & Birmingham shows why the 1834 Bill had called into public question the assault of capital on 'private interests', which was endemic in the 'Railway Mania', and was in its extent an entirely new phenomenon in Britain. The huge numbers of Bills for railways in the 1830s and beyond meant that the compulsory takeover of land became a common feature in England; Great Western companies put forward 36 Bills in the 1830s and 147 from 1840 to 1846. Little evidence appears to exist, however, of the processes involved, although illustration is given by the history of the Syston & Peterborough Railway. While this railway was founded shortly after the main period of railway incorporation, the evidence does show some of the reaction of landowners to the coming of railways. These, with Parliamentary sanction, were setting 'public good' above their 'private interests'.

The railway was authorised on 30 June 1845, and constituted an attempt by George Hudson to secure Peterborough and the Fens for the Midland Railway via the Eastern Counties Railway. There were running battles at Stapleford Park near Oakham as Lord Harborough's retainers impeded the surveyors. When a tunnel under his Cuckoo Plantation fell in, destroying 60 trees, he brought an action against the Midland Railway, sponsors of the line. His men delayed a deviation subsequently authorised on 22 July 1847, by preventing the digging of a cutting. The Midland unsuccessfully sued a hundred of his men for assault.

Some impression of the manner in which the surveying of land prior to construction was affecting landowners is recorded in the biography of Brunel written by his son, which illustrates the dread landowners must have felt at the arrival of the railway engineer or surveyor. His son records that although Brunel had a team of men working for him, nevertheless he was not good at delegating responsibility:

'His own duty of superintendence severely taxed his great powers of work. He spent several weeks travelling from place to place by night, and riding about the country by day, directing his assistants and endeavouring, very frequently without success, to conciliate the landowners on whose property he proposed to trespass... He wrote, "...it is harder work than I like. I am rarely much under twenty hours a day at it."'

In addition to Driver, the Great Western employed J. P. Sturge as its surveyor. He gave evidence to the House of Lords Committee on the Bill in 1835, and that evidence is illustrative of a trend that was to be widespread in England during the 'Railway Mania', of railways being engineered, as one would expect, to take the most direct route with the least engineering problems, and therefore dissecting farms, etc. His evidence also illustrates the processes involved in assessing the value of land to be taken for railways.

He told the Committee that he had valued land for the company between the east of Berkshire and Bristol. His total valuation for land and buildings was £33,593, excluding any houses in Bath. He considered his estimate 'quite a full one', telling the Committee that he had accorded land a value double its sale value, particularly in Christian Malford, the land of the Earl of Carnarvon.

It was pointed out to Sturge that the railway would cut directly through farms in the parish of Christian Malford. He replied he had always endeavoured to establish where boundary lines of particular units of property were, but the difficulty in Christian Malford was the size of some of the farms through which the line was to go. The land there was good arable land used for pasture and meadow, and was not 'wet and spongy'.

Sturge told the Committee that the communications the company proposed to build over or under the line for farms dissected by it – paths and bridges – would reduce its impact, although he acknowledged that it would not 'be so convenient as if the railway was not there, but that would depend upon the number of communications'. Sturge told the Committee he had allowed for building fences in his compensation figures.

The next stage in taking land for the construction of railways was the serving of Notices to Quit. These were issued by the company's solicitors, Osborne Ward, and were signed, in the case of the land at Christian Malford, by George Jones, a director of the company. This Notice set out how serious an impact on rural life the coming of railways was to have. It stated that the railway

> '...will pass through certain meadows, gravel pits, arable fields, footpath, cottages, gardens, parish road, pasture field, ponds, green lanes, brooks, garden grounds, arable common field, nursery, orchard, rick yard and premises situated in the Parish of Christian Malford as set out in the Book of Reference and marked upon a plan deposited with the Clerk of the Peace.'

The Notice threatened that

> '...if for the space of twenty-one days after this notice you shall neglect or refuse to treat or shall not agree with the said company for the sale, conveyance and release of your respected estates or interest ... so required as aforesaid, and also for compensation for any damage sustained by you by reason of the taking of the same ... the said company will by virtue of the powers ... of the said Act issue a Warrant ... commanding the Sheriff of the said County to summon, impanel, and return a jury to inquire of, assess, ascertain, and give a verdict for the sum of money to be paid for the purchase of such hereditament.'

The Great Western provided an estimate of the land to be taken, 21 acres, at £63 an acre, its 'present marketable value'. The cost was based upon an average of the rental value for the previous eight years, to avoid 'an unfair advantage' to the company; this would add 50 per cent to the value of the land, becoming £1,985 for the 21 acres. Separate accounts were made up for each of the tenants of the Earl's estate, and the Carnarvon papers therefore provide an important illustration of the effects of railway promotion on the English countryside, of the processes of land valuation and the relationship the railway companies had to develop with landowners.

Interesting parallels to the Great Western's spending are offered by the Eastern Counties Railway, which was 126 miles long, against the Great Western's 117. Richard Hall, the Eastern Counties' Manager, told the Select Committee on Railways on 7 May 1839 that his company had spent £171,000 on land and compensation. This illustrates how costly a tract of country the Great Western ran through: the Eastern Counties paid £1,357 a mile for land and compensation, the Great Western £1,880 (38.5 per cent more). In fact, according to the details of expenditure laid before the proprietors of the Great Western by the Board at its 19th half-yearly General Meeting on 11 January 1845, the actual cost of construction to 30 June 1844 had been £6,705,153 (£57,309 per mile). Land purchase and compensation was therefore clearly a major capital expense. The Great Western had had to take 2,359 properties, at an average cost of £93.24 each (£5,555 at today's prices), while the Eastern Counties was authorised to take only 1,219 properties in its parent Act. Thus it is evident that the Great Western was to pass through a much more densely settled area of the country than the Eastern Counties.

The 1839 Select Committee on Railways was told by Henry Bosanquet, the Chairman of the Eastern Counties, that he had estimated £150 to £200 an acre for the purchase of land, but that 'the land has no doubt cost a great deal more than was estimated'. As has been observed, such a large difference between estimated and actual cost was by no means unusual.

THE GREAT WESTERN BOOK OF REFERENCE FOR THE 1835 ACT

Petitioning expressed the novelty of railways as invaders of private property, albeit in the interests of what the promoters of railways always described as a greater 'public good'. This caused a large degree of opposition to the Great Western, which was expressed in petitioning of Parliament. Promoters argued that the 'public good' at the heart of their proposed lines of railways should over-ride 'private interests'. This conflict was particularly acute in the Great Western's case because of the number of separate properties that would need to be compulsorily purchased under the Act of incorporation. As the 1834 Bill did not receive Royal Assent, and Parliament was destroyed by fire soon after that Bill's defeat, no manuscript text of it has been preserved in the House of Lords Record Office, and no Bills from this period were printed. However, separate units of property to be purchased are listed in the Book of Reference for the 1835 Act, and in the Schedule of that Act. Every Private Act that involved the compulsory purchase of private property had appended to it such a Book of Reference, listing the owner or reputed owner, the lessee, the occupier, and a brief description of the property to be taken. The geographical distribution of these in the Great Western's case is set out in Table 13, drawn from the 1835 Book of Reference and the Schedule to that Act.

The Book of Reference shows that 2,359 separate units were to be taken, which

City of Bristol	15
County of Somerset	808
County of Gloucestershire	152
County of Wiltshire	1,070
Berks and Wilts	23
County of Berkshire	169
County of Oxfordshire	45
County of Buckinghamshire	19
County of Middlesex	58
Total	**2,359**

Table 13: Units of property
to be taken for the Great Western

explains why the 1834 Bill had called into public question in Parliament the assault on 'private interests'. Members of Parliament in the Reform Bill climate were displaying a new sensitivity to the interests of their constituents.

One of the tasks promoters had to perform, which was imposed by Parliamentary Committees, was that of serving notices on landowners whose property Parliament had given to the promoters of a Bill or whose property was in the draft of the Schedule of the Bill. The scale of this was enormous, far bigger than anything in the canal period. Professor Simmons has observed that it was a vast project to build a railway from London to Bristol, and while this was not necessarily true in the geographical sense, it certainly was in the property sense. Parliamentary Committees became very interested in the question of the practicalities of serving all the notices upon landowners. A House of Lords Select Committee drew attention to the difficulty of the requirement, particularly if the promoters simply could not find the person upon whom physically to serve the notice. Failure to do so was common, and was often used by the opponents of Bills to have them thrown out by Parliament on the grounds of non-compliance with the Standing Orders. As a result, the House of Lords Committee recommended that it should be regarded as adequate simply to post a notice in a prominent location near the affected property (postage stamps were not introduced until 1840):

> '...it has been proved to the Committee that a large amount of expense is incurred by the service of the notices on landowners living at a distance from the line of railway. With a view to meet this difficulty, the Committee endeavoured to ascertain how far it might be possible to provide for the due performance of this service by means of the system of registered letters. It appears, however, from the Evidence of Blott, an officer of experience in the department of the Post Office, that there would be insuperable obstacles to the attainment of that object, from the inadequacy of the establishment, both in town and country, to the proposed duty.'

Thus the Great Western proposal was a great deal more contentious than those for other railways, and the Book of Reference shows a fundamental reason for this: the railway was proposed to pass through a densely settled part of Great Britain, and presumed a considerably greater take-over of private property per mile than did other railways.

REACTIONS TO THE GREAT WESTERN: INSTITUTIONS

Eton College

One of the leading examples of non-private opposition to the Great Western Bill in 1834 was Eton College, an opposition fully expressed in Parliament, and the tone of which illustrated the conflict between public and private interests evidenced by the Great Western Railway's Bills. The Provost of Eton, Dr Goodall, told a public meeting that the College 'would endeavour to prevent it [the railway] to the utmost of their abilities and to the extent of their purse'. He told the Meeting that no 'public good' whatever could possibly come from such an undertaking, and he should be wanting in his duty to the establishment over which he presided if he did not oppose it to the utmost of his ability.

The College received the support of the *Berkshire Gazette*, which said on 10 January 1834 that 'foremost among the enemies of the Bill were the authorities of Eton College which has been and will, I hope, ever be the fostering-mother of almost all the aristocracy of wealth and birth that proud England can boast of.' The Earl of Kerry, seconding the motion in the

Commons for the second reading of the Bill, regretted that 'some opposition was made to this Bill by a learned body, the Provost and Fellows of Eton College'. He drew attention to the fact that the railway was proposed to come within a mile and a half of the College, but 'the Governors of Harrow and Rugby, within a quarter of a mile of which the Birmingham Railroad would pass, had not objected to that'.

Charles Russell, MP for Reading, said that assertions of damage to the boys of the College

'...appeared to him most preposterous. No man could take a greater pride than he did in such a noble institution as that, but could it be seriously contended that they were to stand in the way of a great national work?... Would it not be more reasonable, instead of listening to the fears and complaints of the masters, to exact from them more vigilance and caution? After all, the question at issue was, are the advantages to the public from the construction of the railway sufficient to counter-balance the evils of a partial invasion of private property?'

The Lords Committee was told by Dr Hawtrey, the new headmaster of the College, that

'...we conceive the railway will give the boys the facility between every school-time of running up to London and back again in the hours they have to themselves... It would be impossible to keep the boys from the railway. Anybody who knows the nature of boys, or of Eton boys, will agree in that.'

Henry Labouchère, Liberal Member for Taunton, scorned the College's Petition:

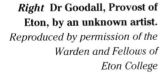

Above right **Dr Hawtrey, headmaster of Eton College, by Helen Scillet.** *Reproduced by permission of the Warden and Fellows of Eton College*

Right **Dr Goodall, Provost of Eton, by an unknown artist.** *Reproduced by permission of the Warden and Fellows of Eton College*

'...anything more preposterous than the assertions made in the Petition from the College that it will be detrimental to the morals of the youths educated there if such a Railroad were within a mile and a half of them he had never heard.'

When the Bill went up to the Lords for its second reading in 1835, the College organised its opposition, but only partially. The Duke of Buccleuch, presenting the Petition of the Provost and Fellows, said 'some doubts having been entertained as to whether the Provost and Fellows of Eton had or had not withdrawn their opposition to the measure, I can now state that they have not.'

Lord Wharncliffe, who again moved the second reading for the company, said he had a letter from the Provost of Eton, 'who informs me that the Provost and Fellows were drawn into the opposition which they originally gave to this measure by false statements that are now proved to be wholly without foundation.' The Duke of Buccleuch, however, said that he had seen Dr Hawtrey the day before, and 'that it is upon his authority that I state that the opposition of the College is not withdrawn'. He went on 'that as regards the original objections of the College – that the railroad would interfere with their property – that was removed by the individuals interested in the Bill entering into an arrangement not to carry a branch to Windsor.' Nevertheless, the College authorities did see the advantages of the railway when it opened, despite their opposition to it. They unsuccessfully tried in the Court of Chancery to stop construction in June 1836, but subsequently commissioned a special train to take pupils to Queen Victoria's Coronation.

Nonetheless, in response to pressure from the College in 1834 the Great Western inserted clauses into the 1835 Bill compelling it or any other company not to make a Branch through Eton, not to build a depot within 3 miles of the College, and to build a fence on each side of the line for 4 miles through certain parishes near Eton. Such clauses were not unprecedented: for example, the Earl of Carnarvon had had such a clause inserted in the Bill for the Wilts & Berks Canal to prevent it interfering with a stream affecting the land of one of his tenants at Christian Malford.

Oxford University

Similar concerns to those of Eton College at the possible effect of railways on young men were felt by the authorities of Oxford University. Brunel was asked by the Committee on the Oxford & Great Western Union Railway Bill in 1838 if he had estimated the number of students of the University who would use the railway to travel up to London, and he said he had not.

Nevertheless, the ultimate Parliamentary sanction for the Great Western's access into Oxford, the Oxford Railway Act of 1843, contained provisions similar to those that the authorities of Eton College had obtained. Thus clause 305 of the Act stipulated that if any Officer of the University should require a railway official not to convey somebody who did not have an MA, the company should not do so, on pain of a fine of £5, whether the person had paid the fare or not. However, the company was excused from reimbursing the passenger who had thus flouted the Act. The University was to appoint Special Constables to superintend this provision.

Such opposition to the railways was by no means common. Towns along the line of the route almost invariably petitioned in favour of a railway, for the obvious boost to trade and communication it would give. This can be seen in the Petitions relating to the Great Western itself, the North Midland, and many other railways. Oxford was, however, a notable exception.

The Commons Journal for 1837-8 records that there was just one Petition in favour of the Bill, while Petitions against were more numerous, coming from the Chancellor, Master and Scholars of the University; inhabitants of Oxford; and the owners of property in Abingdon.

Most unusually, the Corporations of Oxford and of Abingdon also petitioned against the Bill: in the majority of cases town corporations petitioned Parliament in favour of proposals to build a railway for their town. Petitions in favour were confined to one from the inhabitants of Oxford, although, as has been seen, there was also a petition against from this source. The University's Petition revealed the 'town/gown' divide: the Petitioners felt 'satisfied' that existing means of communication were adequate for the purposes of trade in addition to the conveyance of passengers to London. As with the opposition of Eton, the University was concerned that the railway would be 'extremely injurious to the discipline of the University'.

The projected work had 'not originated in the wants and wishes of the inhabitants of Oxford, but has been pressed on them in a great measure by strangers unconnected with its interests ... in a spirit of mere speculation.' The Petition was issued under the Common Seal of the House of Convocation on 19 March 1838. The Commons Committee on the Bill in 1838 heard evidence from a number of non-University inhabitants of Oxford, which showed clearly that the University's Petition was not speaking, as it claimed, for the people of Oxford. William Hemming, the Secretary of the company, told the Committee that those assenting to the Bill owned land on 7 miles and 4 chains of the 9 miles 5 chains route between Oxford and Didcot. Brunel, engineer to the Oxford & Great Western company, told the Committee that the proposal was 'of very great importance' to the public. This was flatly contradicted by the Petition of the University referred to above.

The Minutes of the Hebdomadal Board of the University of Oxford of 26 March 1838 record that the City of Oxford had proposed that it and the University should jointly defray the cost of opposition, but that the Board determined that 'it will be more efficacious to the interests of each body to employ their own Counsel in opposition'. Ultimately, on 29 October, the Minutes record that the Vice-Chancellor reported that the opposition of the University had been successful, and that the Bill had been thrown out by the Committee in the Lords. However, only a year later the Great Western obtained its much sought-after access into Oxford with the Oxford Railway Act, which had been proposed in the company's first prospectus in 1833.

REACTIONS TO THE GREAT WESTERN: INDIVIDUAL LANDOWNERS

The Earl of Carnarvon

It is difficult to obtain detail on the Great Western's negotiations with particular landowners. The largest number of any single individual's units of property projected to be taken by the Great Western was that of the Earl of Clarendon. Unfortunately, his papers at the Bodleian Library offer no detail on the Earl's dealings with the Great Western in 1834 and 1835.

However, those of the 3rd Earl of Carnarvon (1800-1894) illustrate the take-over of the properties of large landed proprietors by railway companies, and were kindly made available to the present author by his descendant, the 7th Earl. These papers contain various items about his ancestor's dealings with the Great Western Railway in the aftermath of the 1835 Act, and provide a useful illustration of the processes involved.

The 1835 Act listed in its Schedule property of his to be taken in the parish of Christian Malford. This comprised 17 units, occupied by 11 people, and variously described as 'cottage and gardens', pasture land, and a hay rick. The surveyor of the Great Western, J. P. Sturge, had prepared a report for the Great Western on the effect of the passing of the railway through the Earl's estates, which stated that the land was 'of the first quality, either for fatting or dairying'. The Great Western was projected to pass through the parish for 2⅜ miles, and would divide some of the farms, in respect of which a 'consideration' would be required of the Great

The 3rd Earl of Carnarvon, by J. E. Collins.
Reproduced by courtesy of the 7th Earl of Carnarvon

Western. Concern was also expressed about the effect of the Great Western upon drainage, and the need for an archway or communication for stock to pass from one part of a farm to that on the other side of the Great Western. Sturge reported that:

> '...heavy damages are the only alternative the proprietor will have to obtain anything like compensation for the injury done to the estate.'

Berkshire landowners

An account of the reaction of landowners in Berkshire to the coming of the railway illustrates the reaction to the advent of railways across the country. These assessments of the reaction are drawn from two local newspapers, the *Mercury*, a Liberal newspaper that supported the Great Western Railway, and the *Chronicle*, a Conservative newspaper that opposed it.

A meeting was held in Reading to promote the railway, followed by a meeting at Windsor at which, according to the *Chronicle*'s report of 12 October 1833,

> '...it was unanimously resolved that the general committee be instructed and empowered to take all such steps as they shall deem advisable for effectually opposing the progress of this useless and mischievous project.'

Conversely, the enthusiasm with which local towns along the line of the route regarded the prospect of the railway can be gauged from the report of the Reading *Mercury* on the appearance of the Great Western's 1833 prospectus, on 30 September. The report highlighted the estimated cost of construction, and observed that it would take four or five years. It enthused that the number of travellers would be multiplied and the manufacture and conveyance of goods enhanced.

Saunders, as the Great Western's Secretary, addressed a meeting in the Town Hall in Reading on 6 March 1834. He told it that:

> 'The situation of Reading has rendered it a very favourite place of resort and the influx of strangers cannot but be increased if the town is brought within an hour and a half or two hours of London, instead of four and a half to five hours. Will not houses be increased in value by the accession of a great number of persons in easy circumstances? The land around the town may be cut up; it will not be by the railway but with villas which will spring up in all directions. And, if the facility of travelling enables such persons as have been mentioned to come and live here, will it be of no advantage to the town to see those beautiful mansions – many of which are now untenanted – filled, as they will be if we can ensure a mode of conveyance expeditious, secure, without fatigue and cheap?'

However, the promoters of the Great Western were disingenuous or short-sighted in their public assessments of the effect of the Great Western upon traffic on the River Thames. Saunders told the Reading meeting that

> '…it has been said that the trade of the Thames will be annihilated … but I believe that the railway will not do any injury to the Thames. The railway is principally for passengers, but if there should be any obstructions to the river navigation, such as frost and drought, then the railway will come to the aid of the river trade. The inns and hotels will be much more frequented from the vast influx of visitors.'

A correspondent stated that

> '…the Thames Commissioners have no right to spend public money opposing another scheme of internal communication, and the only effective opposition would be the improvement of the Thames Navigation by shortening it with canals.'

Clearly, the question of the public advantage that would accrue from the construction of the railway, and which was to lead to the almost immediate bankruptcy of the Kennet & Avon Canal when the Great Western opened, was regarded as superior to the 'private interests' of, in this case, the Thames Commissioners. The effect on the latter, despite Saunders's assurances, was as catastrophic as for the Kennet & Avon Canal: the decline in trade on the River Thames after the opening meant that by 1866 the Thames Commissioners were £900,000 in debt, and were disbanded, control of the River Thames being handed over to the Thames Conservators. In the same way, within ten years of the opening of the railways nearly every turnpike trust was bankrupt.

The Bristol & Exeter and two individual landowners

Further west, on 19 May 1836, the Bristol & Exeter Act received its Royal Assent 'for making a railway from Bristol to Exeter, with branches to the towns of Bridgewater in the county of Somerset and Tiverton in the county of Devon.'

The Schedule of the Act listed the units of property owned by Colonel Tynte that were to be taken: these were a farmhouse, orchards, barns, a coppice, a brook, and pastures in the parishes of Chelvey and Bridgwater, and amounted to 11 acres. Sturge wrote to the Secretary of the Bristol & Exeter on 21 November 1837 reporting that he had had disagreements with Colonel Tynte as to the value of his land. Sturge valued the land at £1,090, while Colonel Tynte valued it at £1,300. The Bristol & Exeter's Board resolved to offer him £1,200 'in full compensation', and the company also offered to build a bridge over the turnpike road on the estate. Colonel Tynte accepted the offer in November 1837.

Sir John Slade (1762-1859) had commanded a Hussar Brigade and Brigade of Dragoons in the Peninsular War (1809-13). He was created a baronet in 1831 and became a general in 1837. Sir John was to lose property under the Bristol & Exeter's proposals in the parish of Bridgwater, consisting of four orchards, cottages and houses, and various farm buildings. Sir John wrote to the Bristol & Exeter company on 28 February 1838 stating that his objection to the line going through his property 'can never be removed', but he was not actuated by 'factious' feelings, and therefore agreed to withdraw his opposition on two conditions: first, on being paid £1,000 at once in addition to the value of the land; and second, the company was not to exercise its Parliamentary power to deviate from the line laid down in the plans submitted to Parliament beyond the 100 yards the Bill authorised, as this would be 'a serious injury' to Sir John's 'comfort', and his principal place of residence.

The Bristol & Exeter's Board resolved to pay the £1,000 and to enter into an Agreement to pay besides for the land when required for the railway as per the Act of Incorporation, and that the Secretary should write forthwith to Sir John to that effect.

ASSESSING LAND VALUES

The methods for the assessment of the value of land were covered by the evidence of Edward Driver, the Great Western's surveyor in 1834, who told the Lords Committee on Compensation that the Great Western had needed 190 acres of land between London and Maidenhead in 1834. His account of how he assessed values offers an important illustration of a process going on all over the country during the 'Railway Mania' of the 1830s:

> 'My mode … is to charge the land first at the full rent; if it is worth 35s an acre, I should call it 40s an acre. I then put it at thirty-three years purchase. I add a fourth to that for compulsory sale, making forty-one years and a half. Then I find a moiety more must be added, making sixteen years and a half purchase more, to cover severance, which makes fifty-eight years purchase; and I have generally said that it comes to sixty years purchase to cover everything.'

The Committee considered that land and land compensation were small parts of the cost of promoting and building a railway and that high land prices did not discourage speculation:

> 'It is also to be observed that the price of the land purchased, and the compensation for that which is injured, form together but a small portion of the sum required for the construction of a railway, so that no apprehension need be entertained of discouraging their formation by calling upon the speculators to pay largely for the rights which they acquire over the property of others.'

However, to 30 June 1844 the Great Western had spent £754,459 on land (£44,870,694 at present-day prices), rather more than a 'small portion'. In addition, the Committee drew attention to land often not being a source of income, but having been the 'subject of expensive embellishment'.

The following extract from the Committee's report serves as a good summary of the conflict of interests that was so characteristic of the railway revolution of the 1830s:

> 'Public advantage may require all these private considerations to be sacrificed, not as it is the only ground upon which a man can be justly deprived of his property and enjoyment, so, in the case of railways, though the public may be considered ultimately the gainers, the immediate motive to their construction is the interest of the speculators, who have no right to complain of being obliged to purchase, at a somewhat high rate, the means of carrying on their speculation.'

The Committee also made a recommendation on the cost of appearing to contest private legislation, a subject that was raised during the debate on the Great Western Bill in 1834. It proposed that

'...when any party contests a Bill before the Committees of the House, the Committee should have power to insist that the whole or part of their costs be borne by the promoters of the Bill.'

Driver had also valued on the Brighton line, and was 'quite satisfied that this mode of calculation would ensure full justice to the landowners, without producing any fancy value or extravagant demands.' The Committee asked whether the price a railway paid for land and property should reflect the level of profits it expected to derive therefrom. Driver replied that he had

'...always reprobated any such notion. I never would allow any argument of that kind to be used ... it has always been held that the advantages from a canal or any such speculative undertaking were never to be taken into consideration in the reduction of the compensation for the land they have taken; therefore I never would submit that.'

He was asked 'if small proprietors have generally been underpaid?'

'I do not think any of them have been underpaid. I do not think there has been any case which I have settled in which I have not conscientiously believed that I paid more than the value and damage.'

He immediately went on to show that he was very much a railway man: asked if 'landowners suffered whilst work was being carried out', Driver replied:

'I do not think they have, because if they have suffered from their hedges being destroyed or anything of that sort, it must be very trifling in comparison with the price they have received for their land; it cannot be worth a moment's consideration in point of money.'

He thought 'most conscientiously' that landowners had got a fair price from his assessments of value, but that landowners had endeavoured to obtain unreasonable sums in compensation. This is borne out by the fact that the Great Western had no juries to decide upon a fair valuation of land along its route.

The landowners in any case were not above trying to exploit the railway revolution to obtain unfair amounts of money for their property because it might be necessary for a railway's planned route. Driver described a case of a landowner who owned 8 acres of land along a projected line of railway to be engineered by Brunel. This landowner had told Driver the price of the property would be £15,000. This was for 'eight acres of mere agricultural land'. This Driver described as 'the sort of exorbitant claim that railway proprietors are often obliged under certain circumstances to comply with.'

The Committee was, of course, taking evidence 12 years after the first Great Western Bill, and asked Driver whether 'there was more opposition then to the sale of land for railway purposes than there is now?' Driver agreed that there had been, but said that he had 'wanted to pay the full fair price for everything. We had only two juries in the whole of the distance between London and Maidenhead.' The Great Western was paying approximately double the value of land to secure an easy passage. Thus Driver told the Committee that the 190 acres of land taken between London and Maidenhead in 1834 had been valued at £200 per acre.

Driver told the Committee that the Great Western had not taken any houses in its proposed line down to Maidenhead. He was asked about the relative fortunes in terms of valuation of the owners of large and small properties:

> 'Small proprietors did get the full value of their land/houses, but the large proprietors, who formerly had more influence than they have had in the last few years, got much more than they ought to have done.'

REACTIONS TO THE GREAT WESTERN:
EXISTING TRANSPORT PROVIDERS

In addition to the effect of the development of railways on the landowners whose property would be needed to effect their construction, another important source of opposition was the owners of existing means of communication. These were likely to lose business to the railways and, indeed, their deficiencies were projected by the promoters of railways as a factor in favour of their schemes.

Railways were unprecedentedly substantial enterprises and, as the passenger figures for both the Great Western and the London & Birmingham demonstrate, became huge carriers of passengers. The two competing means of transport in the 1830s were water (canals and navigable rivers) and roads, principally turnpike trusts. The history of the effect of the Great Western on these in the West of England illustrates effects experienced over much of England.

On 9 December 1833 more than 30 landowners in Berkshire held a meeting at the Bear Inn in Reading. The Secretary of the Thames Commissioners also attended, and he claimed that landowners had not assented to the Bill, despite the Great Western's claims; he got them each to separately deny their assent at this meeting. He told the meeting that the problems included

> '...the destruction of land, the asseverance of enclosures, the inundation of foreign labourers and the increased poor-rate.'

Robert Palmer, the Member of Parliament for Berkshire, told the meeting that the 'line would destroy some of his best farms and divide his estate in 7 different places… [However]; private feelings must yield to the public good.' The meeting resolved that the railway would be

> '...injurious to their [the landowners'] interest, repugnant to their feelings, and that no case of public utility had been made out to justify such an uncalled for encroachment on the rights of private property.'

The newspaper went on to report that the Thames Commissioners and their unfortunate Secretary were objects for scathing criticism:

> 'Secretary Payne is driven to his wits end to make out a case to justify this pernicious opposition to the projected railway. There must be as much public utility in a railway as in a turnpike road or a canal or a river made navigable… The proposed undertaking is fraught with almost incalculable good to the nation and particularly along the line of its operation, by bringing an immense power of capital and industry into mutual co-operation.'

The main transport route to the West of England in 1830 was the Kennet & Avon Canal. This drew, like the Great Western, from Bristol's importance, which continued to grow throughout the Middle Ages as the prosperity of the merchants increased. In 1660 four Bills had been put forward to make the Avon navigable, and in 1712 the Corporation of Bristol had petitioned for a Bill, which was opposed by 16 Petitions. Historian Daphne Philips cites the words of a Reading diarist, setting out the problems traders were facing with using canals and rivers for the trans-shipment of goods: boats from London had not been able to get through for over a month and grocers were employing wagoners to fetch goods by road. The wagons were charging 2s 6d per cwt, whereas the usual charge by water was 11d per cwt. Given dissatisfaction of this sort in Reading, which illustrates the brake that poor communications were putting on the development of the Industrial Revolution in England in the early part of the 19th century, it is unsurprising that the effect of the opening of the Great Western's entire line on 30 June 1841 was, as the Great Western had foreseen in its promotion of its Bill in Parliament, devastating for the Kennet & Avon Canal. Receipts fell from £51,174 in 1840-1 to £19,936 in 1841-2.

The effect of the development of railways on turnpike roads can be illustrated by the effect of the Great Western on turnpikes in Oxfordshire. Author Alan Rosevear comments that the decline one might logically presume to have occurred in turnpike trusts did not do so uniformly. Such a decline was experienced on major trunk routes: thus the number of coaches on the road through Oxford to Birmingham fell from nine to two per day, with no inside passengers. Tolls paid by the coaches on the 'Parliamentary Road' to Birmingham through Coventry fell by £20,000 in the first three years of railway operation. Toll income on the major roads across the Thames Valley suffered a massive drop. Just as the Kennet & Avon Canal had sought to cut its costs, so the lessee of the tolls on the Stokenchurch Turnpike applied for a reduction of his rent, a requirement he attributed directly to the Great Western.

In contrast to canal companies, some turnpikes did, however, benefit to some extent from the railway. Thus the Wallingford, Wantage & Faringdon, which ran alongside the railway through Berkshire, found itself heavily used by passengers travelling to the new stations. Equally, the Rosseleigh Trust had been in a parlous financial state, but the boost of income from traffic to the station made it financially sound. Rosevear concludes that 'it is clear that the coming of the railways was not a disaster for all road transport, nor some of the turnpike trusts. Although the great trunk routes did go into terminal decline after 1840, the general increase in economic activity stimulated by the new method of transport and resulting expansion in local traffic gave new life and purpose to the turnpikes across the Vale of the White Horse.'

Evidence of the mutual benefits to be derived by both railway companies and carriers from the trans-shipment of goods was given to the Select Committee on Railways on 15 March 1844 by Charles Saunders. He was asked by the Committee about various aspects of the company weighing goods for transportation, and cited an agreement signed between the company and Messrs Pickford & Co, under which the company would pay Pickford's 10 per cent of the charge to be levied on goods brought by them to the railway for forward transmission by the railway.

10.

RAILWAY SHAREHOLDERS AND THE PROMOTION OF RAILWAYS

'Mr Heyworth (of Liverpool) said the errors into which Mr Brunel had fallen were not trifling for, acceding to his opinion, it had taken out of his pocket no less than £70,000. It had been said that those who took the same view that he did were mischievous. What had been the result of that mischief, as it had been called? Why, a saving, by the abandonment of the piles alone, of £48,000 (cheers). Large sums were expended on machinery and works that would not succeed (cheers). It would be much better to suspend the laying of rails on the wide gauge.'

Bristol Mercury, *12 January 1838*

THE EFFECT OF FINANCIAL STABILITY

The Great Western was developing through the acquisition or lease of other companies, but it was also building its own new mileage. As has been seen above, the company opened for business from London to Maidenhead on 4 June 1838, and by 17 December 1840 had reached Hay Lane, between Swindon and Wootton Bassett. The line opened throughout on 30 June 1841, with the completion of the most significant engineering work on the route, Box Tunnel. The 1830s was a period of virtually no inflation, a factor that encouraged speculation in the new phenomenon of railways. However, the price of a Great Western share in 1835 was £100, the equivalent of £5,947 today, so although railways were spreading share ownership in a way canals certainly had not, with the latter's statutory limitations on the numbers of shareholders, the high price meant that they were not making share ownership available to the lower classes of society.

As has been seen, the driving force in the Great Western and its expansion was Brunel: his visionary espousal of the broad gauge meant that the Great Western's capital base expanded considerably to fuel his ideas. Table 14 sets out the different issues of shares made by the Great Western, the funds from which flowed principally into the expansion of the company through lease and purchase. The company also, of course, received loan-raising powers under the Acts, allowing it to create shares that, as was standard in railway legislation, amounted to half the value of the share-raising powers.

Shareholders did not have to pay the whole value of their shares when they first contracted to buy them. The unused portion of the purchase value could be 'called up' by the company upon resolution of a proprietors' meetings after the initial issue of the new shares. In 1835 prospective Great Western subscribers were required to pay a deposit of £5 for their £100

Table 14: Great Western share capital

Date	Shares		Capital
	Value	Number	
1835	£100	25,000	£2,500,000
1839	£50	25,000	£1,250,000
1840	£20	37,500	£750,000
Totals		**87,500**	**£4,500,000**

Table 15: Liverpool & Manchester share capital

Date	Shares		Capital
	Value	Number	
1824	£100	5,100	£510,000
1829	£25	5,100	£127,500
1831	£25	6,375	£159,375
1837	£50	7,968	£398,400
Totals		**24,543**	**£1,195,275**

shares. Twelve calls were then made over the following years until the full £100 was paid up, in January 1849. The £50 shares created by a resolution of 26 June 1839 also required a deposit of £5, but were fully paid up by 29 December 1840 by five further calls. The 37,500 £20 shares created on 27 August 1840 were paid up in three instalments over a period of three years and three months.

The London & Birmingham also had a capital of £2,500,000, while the York & North Midland had a capital of £370,000, albeit for a distance of only 37½ miles. The Stockton & Darlington had been authorised to raise capital of £100,000 in 1821. The Great Western and the London & Birmingham companies therefore demonstrated a dramatic increase in the levels of capital previously required for Private Bills.

Table 15 shows the share capital raised by the Liverpool & Manchester Railway, providing a context for the Great Western's issues. After 1837 the Liverpool & Manchester created no new share issues until 1845. Incorporated in 1826, the line was only 30¾ miles long, and even after 15 years of development the company's capital was only 67.7 per cent of the Great Western's inaugural capital.

George Hudson's York & North Midland was created with 37,500 shares at £50 each. The deposit was smaller than the Great Western's, at only £1, and the whole £50 was called up in six instalments, to May 1840. The London & Birmingham's shares were sold, like the Great Western's, with a £5 deposit, and were paid up in 12 further instalments by 10 January 1843. That company's proprietors therefore had to pay up six years before the Great Western's, evidence of the extent to which receipts on the Great Western were out-stripping expenses, providing more profit to fund growth. The expansion of the share base of the Great Western, which was so much greater than that of the Midland, indicates once again the driving force of Brunel; it was clearly a much more expansionist line than even Hudson's Midland. Yet for all the principal railways in Great Britain that had been incorporated by the end of 1840, there was good reason for the boom in promotion of the 1840s: working expenses as a percentage of gross traffic receipts were ranging from 24 to 35 per cent.

THE SEALED REGISTER

Three main groups of people were sensitive to the development of railways: their users, landowners, whose reactions were considered in Chapter 9, and those who invested in them. This last group now forms the focus of consideration. Such an analysis was formerly done by Dr M. V. C. Reed in his *Investment in Railways in Britain, 1820-1844*; he bases his analysis of the type of people buying shares in the early railway companies around the manuscript subscription contracts of 1835, and secondly on the Great Western's Sealed Register of proprietors. A similar study has been made of various Lancashire and Yorkshire railways by Seymour Broadbridge, while Dr J. Lee used subscription contracts and company material to analyse the financing of Irish railways.

The sources of the capital actually raised immediately after incorporation in 1835 by – rather than simply promised to – the Great Western are set out in the company's Sealed Register of proprietors. This was a list of all proprietors, and was ordered by the proprietors to have the company seal affixed to it at their meeting of 29 October 1835, hence its name. It lists in numbered alphabetical order each of the 1,443 subscribers, with their places of residence, followed by their occupations and the number of shares actually

bought; the occupations are as given by the proprietors themselves on their Deeds of Contract. The 1,443 proprietors owned 22,911 shares in total, and the average investment in the company was £1,596 (£94,962 at present-day prices). These were indeed huge sums.

The number of occupations in the Sealed Register is 163, and the number of locations in which the proprietors lived is 237. The number of shares bought by individuals ranged from one, bought by 144 individuals, to more than 125, which were bought by 24 people, costing more than £12,500 (£743,429 today). The contributions of these 24 people ranged from £12,500 up to £77,500.

The history of the early financing of the Great Western brings out the fluidity of railway financing at the start of the 'Railway Mania'. The Sealed Register records the contributions of the Bristol Committee soon after incorporation. However, Geoffrey Channon has analysed the contributions of the Committee as recorded in the Deeds of Contract required to be laid before the House of Commons before any Bill could go forward for a second reading. His analysis shows that the members of the Bristol Committee collectively took up £38,700 less in shares by the time of the compilation of the Register.

Only three of the 14 members had increased their subscriptions: Robert Bright, George Gibbs, and George Jones. The clearest reduction in support was by Nicholas Roch, who was nominated as a councillor for the Redcliffe ward in Bristol in 1835, and was a director of Bristol Dock Company from at least 1816, and subsequently of the Port of Bristol Authority. His contribution fell from £23,500 to only £10,000.

The 24 largest proprietors of the company spent in total £471,300 on their shares: 1.7 per cent of proprietors therefore held 20.6 per cent of all the shares, while the 9.2 per cent of proprietors who held one share owned 0.6 per cent of the shares. As has been observed above, Brunel himself bought 80 shares, George Stephenson 50, and Saunders 84. The North Midland Railway's Secretary, Henry Patterson, appeared before his company's House of Commons Committee on 16 March 1836 and explained that his undertaking had sold 11,703 shares to 397 proprietors, 204 of whom had subscribed £2,000 or more. Comparing the average subscriptions brings out the strength of Bristol's commercial wealth: the North Midland's average shareholding was £827, compared to the Great Western's £1,588. However, a Return ordered by Parliament of people spending more than £2,000 on railway shares in all companies in 1846 is marked by the complete absence of Great Western proprietors. This is of significance because the absence of large shareholders among the Great Western's proprietors removed one potential source of difficulty for Brunel in achieving his domination of every aspect of the railway. There was no equivalent of a George Hudson figure among the Great Western's proprietors; indeed, the Return's account of Hudson's spending offers a dramatic contrast, as he spent a total of £818,540 on 23 different schemes, none of them Great Western companies.

The Return records that those spending more than £2,000 on railway shares in 1846 spent £121,255,374 (£6.6 billion at present-day prices); 21 per cent of this total was from people spending more than £100,000 each. The list of those spending more than £100,000 does not include the names of any of the original Great Western directors, although it does include Frederick Ricketts, Chairman of the Bristol & Exeter, and thereby a director of the Great Western after the latter's lease of his company in 1840. He spent £217,650 on seven schemes, one of which was the South Devon, a railway in which the Bristol & Exeter had a substantial stake, one-fifth of its capital of £1,000,000.

This chapter now offers an analysis of the occupational character of those buying shares in the Great Western, based around the Sealed Register of proprietors and analysed by Census categories. Reed has produced a useful occupational distribution of shareholdings in the Great Western, but his analysis is based around very unrefined categories: trade, manufacturing, banking, gentlemen, etc, and land. The method used here of applying contemporary Census categories to the analysis enables the historian to paint a much more defined picture of the Great Western's shareholders in 1835.

The Register offers an invaluable base for a social snapshot of the people who were buying railway shares at the start of the 'Railway Mania'. To draw meaningful data from the Register does, however, pose methodological difficulties, principally because of the number of different occupations – 238 – listed in the subscription contract by the investors. Hollins's analysis of the capital sources for the Liverpool & Manchester Railway concentrates on the geographical origins of the 391 proprietors, who held 2,904 shares. The Great Western's Sealed Register of 1835 showed that the company had 1,443 proprietors in 1835, who held 22,911 shares. The largest contemporary statistical analysis showing occupations was the 1831 Census, which, like the Register, relied upon self-classification for people's occupations, and for the present study the 1831 Census categories have been applied to the Great Western's Sealed Register.

I	Commerce, trade and manufacture
II	Agriculture, as farmers, graziers, agricultural labourers, gardeners, nurserymen, and florists
III	Labour, not agricultural (a miscellaneous group that included miners, guardians, porters and messengers, as well as all those whose employment 'is not otherwise specified')
IV	Army
V	Navy
VI	Professions: clerical, legal, medical
VII	Pursuits followed by 'other educated persons'
VIII	Government (Civil Service)
IX	Municipal and Parochial offices
X	Domestic servants
XI	Persons of independent means
XII	Almspeople, pensioners, paupers, lunatics and prisoners

Table 16: Occupational categories used in the 1831 Census

Census description		% of whole occupied population	% of Great Western proprietors
I	Commerce, trade and manufacture	39.1	33.9
II	Agriculture	18.1	0.8
III	Labour, not agricultural	10.0	0.4
IV	Army, at home	0.55 }	0.8
	Army, Ireland	1.3 }	
V	Navy, at home	1.4 }	0.4
	Navy, afloat	1.4 }	
VI	Professions, clerical	0.3 }	
	Professions, legal	0.2 }	6.1
	Professions, medical	0.3 }	
VII	Pursuits followed by 'other educated persons'	1.8	9.1
VIII	Government (Civil Service)	0.2	0.8
IX	Municipal and Parochial offices	0.3	0.1
X	Domestic servants	14.1	0.8
XI	Persons of independent means	6.7	35.9
XII	Almspeople, pensioners, paupers, lunatics and prisoners	0.3	0

Total population returned as occupied, etc   6,706,920
Remainder of population (including women and children)   9,390,366

Table 17: Great Western proprietors and the
occupied population compared by 1831 Census categories

These categories are as shown in Table 16, and two further categories have been added to enable a complete analysis of the Register to be made:

XIII Illegible
XIV Occupation not given

These two categories provided, respectively, 1.7 and 2.1 per cent of proprietors.

Table 17 compares the percentage of Great Western proprietors in the various Census categories with the percentage those categories constituted of the whole occupied population, while Table 18 shows the percentage of Great Western shareholders and shares in the various categories. It can therefore be seen that the sociological breakdown of the Great Western's investors did not mirror that of the population as a whole in occupational terms.

It is a marked feature that those who may be termed 'old capital', or those of independent means, were substantially over-represented among the Great Western's proprietors compared to their position in the population as a whole: 35.9% compared to 6.7%. The 'new capital' of the Industrial Revolution, which was largely based in areas of the country other than those served by the Great Western (the manufacturing interests), was not making any more than a broadly equal contribution, 39.1% to 33.9%. Seymour Broadbridge (1970) applied occupational categories to 11 different railway companies in Lancashire and Yorkshire, and breaks down his

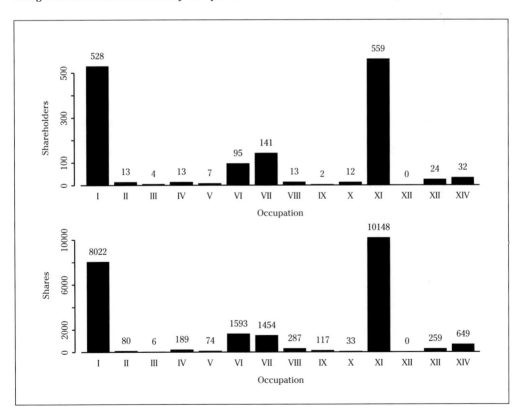

**Table 18: Great Western proprietors and their shareholdings by
1831 Census categories (Source PRO RAIL251/1)**

occupational assessment into six categories, trade, industry, law, land, banking and miscellaneous. His categories have the disadvantage that they are not of contemporary origin and are not as precisely defined as the Census categories of 1831, but nevertheless are of some interest to provide broad context for the assessment here.

On the Liverpool & Manchester companies, the total number of proprietors whom Broadbridge describes as 'gentlemen' and 'land' ranged from 7 per cent on the Bolton & Preston to 30 per cent on the Manchester & Leeds and the Wakefield, Pontefract & Goole. On the Great Western 'gentlemen' and 'esquires' (Class XI occupations in terms of the 1831 Census) constituted 27.33 per cent of proprietors. It is of significance to observe, as for the Great Western figures, the dominance of mercantile rather than manufacturing interests. The Great Western had very limited subscriptions from the manufacturing interests of Birmingham, Manchester and West Yorkshire, emphasising the importance of local capital in financing early railways. The Great Western sold only 65 shares to two subscribers in Birmingham, and 40 shares to four subscribers in Manchester, none of whom were engaged in industry. Only three shares were sold to two subscribers from Leeds, one from Halifax, and none from Bradford. This was despite a Parliamentary Return of 1846 showing that Manchester men were indeed investing heavily in railways: in that year ten Manchester men made an average investment of £210,127 in various railway schemes (£11,467,990 at today's prices). This speculative excitement was an object of great interest to contemporary cartoonists, and it is therefore little surprise that Charles Saunders should have captured such a scene in one of his splendid sketches.

Class I of the 1831 Census categories covered mercantile and trading groups, and in the Sealed Register includes 169 different occupations, including 11 butchers, 10 bakers and one candlestick-maker. It also includes 115 'merchants', who constituted the largest single occupation among the Great Western's proprietors, although they are exceeded in number by those describing themselves as 'gentleman' or 'esquire', which were of course not occupations. These 115 merchants held 5,112 shares (an average of 26.87 each); at present-day prices, they therefore subscribed £159,808 each. Forty-three of them, more than one-third, gave Bristol as their place of residence. Another feature is the number of the 528 Class I shareholders who held small amounts of shares: 103 had only bought one share, and a further 59 had bought fewer than ten. Nevertheless, 356 spent over £1,000 on shares.

Since the Great Western was predominantly financed by 'old' rather than 'new' capital, that is landed wealth rather than the new wealth generated by the Industrial Revolution, Class

'The Railway Share Market continues to wear the same old doleful features': another satirical cartoon by Charles Saunders, c1840. *National Railway Museum, York*

XI (persons of independent means) has more subscribers than any other single Census class, 559 subscribers holding 10,148 shares, who in their subscription contracts described themselves as 'gentleman' or 'esquire', or 'spinster', 'wife' or 'widow' (all women in the Register are classified by their relationship to men). The Register is therefore dominated by two relatively imprecise social classifications, 'gentleman' and 'esquire', which produced 312 (22 per cent) and 129 (9 per cent) of the proprietors respectively. Their heavy representation among the Great Western proprietary is an indication of the wealth the landed classes were accruing at that time, a wealth often expressed in the building of country houses.

Class XI proprietors overall came from a broad area of the country, unlike those of Class I. Twenty-seven different locations were the sources of Class XI shareholdings of more than 100 shares in total. The numbers of Class XI shares is headed by 3,089 sold to London proprietors and 1,135 sold to Bristol proprietors. Only 37 of the 559 Class XI proprietors lived in places not on the route of the Great Western: 20 were from Liverpool, where they had bought an average of 17.8 shares each. Liverpool, like Bristol, had a great mercantile interest in the Great Western, and the 25 proprietors in that class bought an average of 25 shares each, compared to the Bristol merchants' 15.5. Class XI shareholdings were broadly similar, at 18 shares per Class XI proprietor in Liverpool and 18.5 in Bristol. All 24 directors of the Midland Counties Railway in 1836 described themselves as 'esquire' or 'gentleman', and therefore Class XI in 1831 Census terms, whereas, as has been seen, the Great Western's directors were predominantly Class I, merchants. Finally, it is reassuring to find that there were no lunatics among the Great Western's proprietors.

The Sealed Register also records data for the geographical location of the Great Western's 1,443 shareholders and shares in 1835, and an analysis of the locations is set out in Tables 19 and 20. It is more precisely defined than that of Dr Reed, whose account is very broadly based (Scotland, Midlands, East, South West, etc). The method used in this book of analysis of the locations of the proprietors produces 258 different locations. The Great Western Railway had been originally projected in the prospectus of 30 July to 31 December 1833 as the Bristol & London Railway; Bristol was given as their place of residence by 331 proprietors, or 23 per cent, while 278, or 19.3 per cent, gave London. Bristol was the largest single source of proprietors (see Table 20), and the dominance of Class I proprietors is evident, 56.5 per cent of Bristol proprietors being so classified, compared to 33.9 per cent of all proprietors. Class XI is the largest overall Census class of proprietors, at 35.9 per cent, but in Bristol only 18.7 per cent of proprietors were from this category (see Table 21).

Much of the capital, as has been seen, came from towns along the line of the route, and the list for Reading illustrates the character of people buying railway shares in a particular location. The Borough of Reading in the 1831 Census had a population of 15,595 people; of those, 47 different people bought a total of 749 shares in the Great Western, in quantities ranging from one share to the 127 shares bought by Henry Simmonds, a member of a long-established local banking family. Most bought five shares or fewer, although 17 of the 47 on the list bought more than ten shares. A major feature of the professional character of purchasers from Reading, then a small Berkshire market town, is the paucity of proprietors of Class XI ('independent'). There are only nine proprietors of that Class, fewer than 20 per cent, but they had bought 305 of the 749 shares sold to Reading proprietors (40.7 per cent).

The most significant place of origin not in the areas served by the railway was Liverpool, which had 49 proprietors (3.4 per cent) and was the fifth largest source of proprietors. However, in terms of shares it was the third largest, with 4.9 per cent, exceeded only by London, with 27.1 per cent, and Bristol, with 23 per cent. The 372 proprietors who owned fewer than ten shares were located in 239 different places.

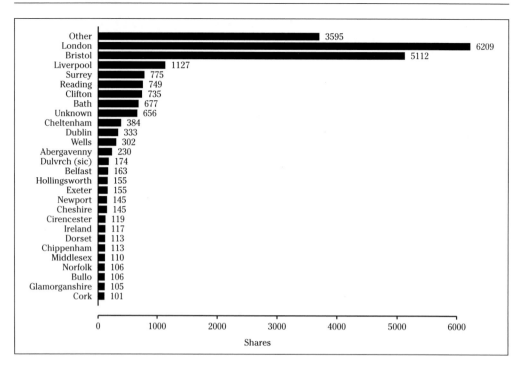

Table 19: Locations holding more than 100 Great Western shares (Source PRO RAIL251/1)

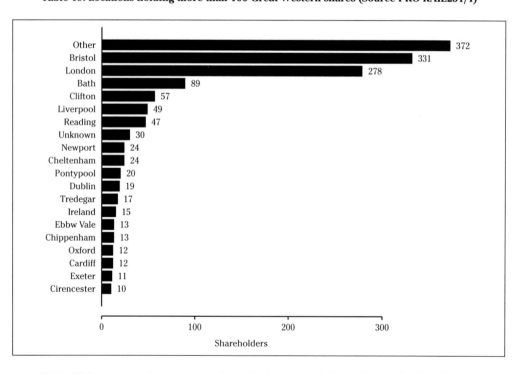

Table 20: Locations with 10 or more Great Western shareholders (Source PRO RAIL251/1)

Table 19 lists the 28 places (including 'other' and 'unknown') that were the source of more than 100 shares, while Table 20 lists the places that were the sources of more than ten proprietors. The locations are those given by the subscribers in their Deeds of Contract, so are unsatisfactory in that there are separate entries for Ireland, Belfast, Cork and Dublin, for example. At the time of the Register's compilation, Clifton was still legally separate from Bristol, as yet unaffected by the provisions of the Municipal Corporations Act of 1835. Nevertheless, the numbers involved are not substantial enough to detract from the overall pattern of the table.

The main distinction between the lists of locations of shares and that of proprietors is that London now exceeds Bristol, even if allowance is made for Clifton being separately listed from Bristol in the subscribers' contracts. Overall, 247 places provided fewer than 300 shares, 231 of which provided fewer than 100 shares. The largest single shareholder in the company was John Woolley from Surrey, a Class XI proprietor holding 775 shares. Most shares therefore came, with the exception of those from Liverpool and Dublin, from places along the line of the route. The Manchester and Liverpool railways similarly drew a substantial portion of shares from towns along the route: Liverpool provided 15 per cent of the capital for the Bolton & Preston and 27 per cent for the Liverpool & Bury. Manchester provided more than 50 per cent of the capital for the Manchester & Leeds, and the Wakefield, Pontefract & Goole. The Manchester and Liverpool railways thus illustrate the driving force of 'new' capital from Lancashire. This Liverpool capital emerged also in the Great Western and the Bristol & Exeter

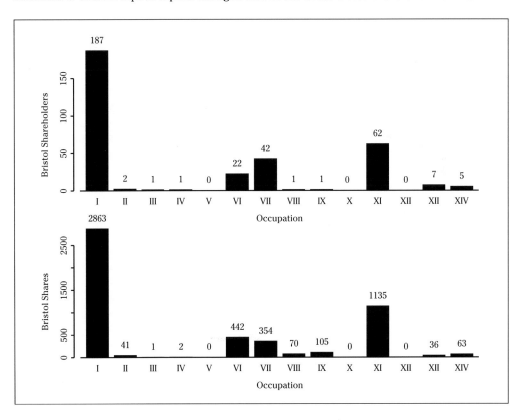

Table 21: Bristol shareholdings by 1831 Census categories (Source PRO RAIL251/1)

companies, but interestingly there were only four Manchester proprietors among the Great Western's proprietary, holding a total of only 48 shares.

Another example of local sources of capital is observable in the case of the Midland Counties Railway. The House of Commons Committee on this Bill met on 18 March 1836, and subjected John Fox Bell, the Secretary of the company, to a detailed examination on the sources of the company's capital. He said that 200 proprietors were 'in the local interest'. Unfortunately for Bell, he had attributed some subscriptions to the 'local interest' that manifestly were not so, and he was rigorously questioned on this point, evidence of how important this issue was to Parliament. Members in the post-Reform Bill era saw the task of representation and protection of the interests of their constituents as of great significance, a feature very evident in the manner of the conduct of Select Committees on Railway Bills. George Hudson told the House of Commons Committee on the York & North Midland Railway Bill in 1836 that a substantial proportion of an authorised capital of £370,000 for that railway had been subscribed locally, in Yorkshire.

Evidence to the House of Lords Committee reflected the local flavour of the capital sources of many railways – as had been the case with the financing of the canals – so the financing of the Great Western was by no means unique during the 'Railway Mania'. For example, local enterprise was the 'keynote' of the Liverpool & Manchester Railway: the total number of names in the Liverpool & Manchester's list of proprietors was 381, of whom 235 came from Liverpool and Manchester themselves (62 per cent). The total number of Liverpool and Manchester shares was 4,233.

'Local interest' was therefore an important factor that railway companies tended to plead before the House of Commons to demonstrate the local significance of and support for their proposed lines of railway. The House of Commons Committee on the North Midland Railway, in 1836, was dominated by a discussion of why the North Midland's secretary, Henry Patterson, had miscalculated the number of assents to the railway from those 'locally interested' along the route. The North Midland Railway was authorised on 4 July 1836, and was engineered by George Stephenson, who laid out a route from Derby to Leeds. The amalgamation of this company with the Midland Counties and the Sheffield & Derby Junction Railway created the Midland Railway on 10 May 1844. Thirty-eight of the North Midland's subscribers had subscribed £5,000 or more, the largest single shareholder being Wood of Manchester, who had subscribed £15,000.

Patterson appeared before the Committee on 16 March, and explained that the company had sold 3,283 shares. He was quizzed on the extent to which those with a 'local interest' had subscribed to the railway. He told the Committee that £782,000 had been thus subscribed. Unfortunately, Patterson had listed as 'locally interested' a tradesman living in Birmingham, and he came under pressure concerning his description of Birmingham as local; the Committee was not satisfied that the shareholder could justly be described as 'locally interested'. Patterson told the Committee that he had listed the subscriber because 'he was so interested in the trade in consequence of his businesses'. That did not satisfy his interrogator: 'Then he is no more locally interested than a button-maker in London would have been, is he?' Patterson ultimately conceded the point: 'Perhaps if I had considered the matter in the way it is now put before me, I might not have put him in.' He told the Committee, 'I have not put in a person trading on the line with the exception of the instances mentioned here.'

More problems lay in store for Patterson when he was asked if he knew where a place was. He said he did not, but the Committee immediately took him to task because he had again placed a subscriber living in that place among those 'locally interested'. He ultimately acknowledged that the offending name, and the £2,000 subscribed, should be transferred to another list. The Committee then fastened on another such error, and finally, exasperated, asked Patterson, 'How happens it that you were employed in making out this list if you have so little information?' Patterson said the list had been 'done rather in a hurry'. He told the Committee he 'must fairly admit that there are errors which have been pointed out in that list which I was not aware of and which I regret appear there.'

Select Committees on many railway Bills were also interested in the level of support for schemes from towns as well as individuals such as those cited here. On occasion, towns that opposed the coming of railways changed their tune, but found the railway companies were not as forthcoming as they had been initially. The case of Abingdon illustrates this. Abingdon had submitted two petitions to Parliament against a railway in 1837 and 1838, but in 1842 the Council consulted Saunders to persuade the company to build the Great Western's Oxford line near to Abingdon, 'for the convenience of the town and its trade'. The Abingdon Council then sent a deputation to a Board meeting of the Great Western, and the company asked it for its agreement to a line from Oxford to Didcot with a branch to Abingdon. The Council refused, four members voting in favour and five not voting. That ended all proposals from the Great Western to build to Abingdon. Eventually a branch was built by the Abingdon Railway Company, opening in 1856, and was ultimately worked by the Great Western from 1904.

One might suppose that the 'new' wealth created by the Industrial Revolution was more sympathetic to the potential of the railway revolution than 'old' wealth, but it was not making a disproportionate contribution to the railway revolution. However, in 1835 the greatest fortunes had not yet been made: William Armstrong built his first piece of hydraulic equipment in 1839; Titus Salt discovered his method of alpaca manufacture in 1836; Samuel Lister's contributions to the development of the worsted industry largely dated from the second half of the 19th century. Additionally, of course, Bristol was not an industrial centre of this revolution in the way Manchester, Bradford and Leeds were, so the relative absence of manufacturing interests from the Great Western's proprietary observed there may be evidence simply of the decline of Bristol after the end of the slave trade in the late 18th century. Additionally, as is observed in this chapter, local support for railways was strong, so one would not have expected those making fortunes from the Industrial Revolution elsewhere in Great Britain to invest in a West Country railway.

THE GREAT WESTERN'S PROPRIETORS: BRUNEL AND THE OPPOSITION OF THE 'LIVERPOOL PARTY'

The geographical origins of the Great Western's capital had direct consequences on the running of the company; in particular it was affected by the activities of what Professor Simmons calls the 'Liverpool Party', that is the company's proprietors from Liverpool. Such a 'Liverpool Party' existed in several other railway companies, according to Professor Simmons: the Midland Counties Railway, its Secretary told the House of Commons Committee on that Bill in 1836, had sold £76,000 of shares in Liverpool. The Board of the Bristol & Exeter heard from its Chairman and some members that they had ascertained 'that of almost every railway that has proceeded with spirit ... two-thirds or upwards of the shares are held by persons living in Lancashire'. The exaggeration shows a certain paranoia about the 'Liverpool Party', but emphasises Liverpool's widespread significance in the promotion of railways.

The diary of Henry Gibbs, one of the inaugural directors of the Great Western, frequently refers to the problems he, Brunel and the directors faced from the Liverpool proprietors of the Great Western. They established an association in the city, and the most dramatic effect they had upon the company was the proposal at a proprietors' meeting of a motion highly critical of Brunel. Brunel's opponents drew 'expert' support from Nicholas Wood and Sir John Hawkshaw, the frequency of whose appearances at the House of Commons before railway Select Committees to advocate the 'narrow' gauge has been observed above.

In response to the concerns expressed by the proprietors, the Board asked Wood and Hawkshaw to prepare a report on Brunel's engineering and its 'peculiar' features. Wood had strong views on the disadvantages of the broad gauge, particularly speed, and carried out experiments to compare the two gauges. The pair came to conclusions in favour of the 'narrow' gauge, to which Brunel responded in a typical manner.

A substantial mythology has grown up around the 'Liverpool Party' in the Great Western Railway. The Sealed Register drawn up by Saunders on 29 October 1835 sets out their contribution as comprising 3.39 per cent of proprietors (49 in number) with 4.92 per cent of the shares (1,127 of the total of 22,911 shares sold in 1835). The Great Western's Act of Incorporation had authorised it to sell 25,000 shares, and while the total actually sold was slightly less than that, the Liverpool figure is substantially below the figure of 20 per cent claimed by some historians – the 49 Liverpool proprietors represented only 3.4 per cent of the total of 1,443. Saunders's letterbook does, however, record an acute sensitivity to the Liverpool proprietors, and it was Laurence Heyworth, a Liverpool merchant who owned 25 shares, who moved a motion to instruct the directors to discontinue the broad gauge. Nevertheless, they were not a significant part of the shareholding in either numbers of proprietors or shares held. Likewise, as has been seen, the Sealed Register shows that the contribution of Manchester to the Great Western's proprietary was tiny, the city providing only four proprietors, holding 48 shares in all.

The effect of the 'Liverpool Party' on the Great Western is detailed in Gibbs's diary, and the conflict between Liverpool and Bristol that was to emerge over the use of the broad gauge originated in the rivalry of the two cities as ports. How important that rivalry was, which the Great Western was projected to obviate, was revealed by evidence given by Mr Adam, counsel for the promoters, to the Committee on the Liverpool & Manchester Railway Bill. He told the Committee that:

> 'Liverpool is the port of England which carries on by much the larger share of intercourse with the United States of America, with South America, with British America, with Ireland, with Africa, and is connected with many other important branches of trade.'

On 1 September 1838 Gibbs reports the Liverpool efforts to secure seats on the Board of the Great Western. He records that he felt

> '...more mortified and disgusted than I can express about the conduct of the Liverpool people with reference to the railway, and I do not know what course to pursue. It seems that they are dissatisfied or pretend to be so, with Mr Brunel ... but the object of all this agitation is evidently to force themselves into the direction.'

Gibbs records the receipt of a letter from the Liverpool proprietors, stating that

> '...we had lost their confidence, and that the only way for the concern to go on at all satisfactorily would be to introduce three Liverpool gentlemen to our direction.'

Gibbs cuttingly observes that 'a greater instance of conceit and vanity I never saw'.

The company did, however, give due weight to its Liverpool proprietors. Thus, when new shares were issued, one of the four banks at which payments could be made was the Bank of Liverpool in that city. The same facility was offered to subscribers to the Bristol & Exeter Railway, despite the distance of Liverpool from the line of that railway. This evidence confirms the importance of Liverpool capital in railway incorporation over the whole of Great Britain.

The Great Western Board Minutes of 27 September 1836 record the receipt from Laurence Heyworth of a resolution passed by the Liverpool Association. This complained that not enough information was being forwarded to them about decisions taken in Bristol and London by the Board.

The most dramatic effect of the origins of capital from, in particular, Liverpool on the development of the company came at the half-yearly meeting of the proprietors on 9 January 1839. As normally happened at these meetings, the directors' half-yearly report to the proprietors was proposed to be approved. The *Bristol Mercury* of 12 January 1839 records that a motion was proposed

'...that this meeting, being deeply sensible of the disastrous consequences inevitably arising from the continued discussion of the principles acted on in carrying out the works, to request the directors to adhere to the principles laid down in their report, as the most conducive to the permanent welfare of the proprietors.'

An amendment was proposed by Heyworth. He moved

'...that the report of Messrs Wood and Hawkshaw contains sufficient evidence that the plans and construction pursued by Mr Brunel are injudicious, expensive, and ineffectual for their professed object, and ought therefore not to be proceeded in.'

By 1846 Wood and Hawkshaw were both prosperous enough to feature in the account of those subscribing more than £2,000 for shares in railway companies during that year. Sir John, listed as a civil engineer, spent £2,500 on two schemes, while Wood is listed as a coal owner, who spent £48,840, also on two schemes. Wood's spending in particular was a huge sum.

Wood had asked to visit the works of the Great Western, on 4 September 1838. Saunders wrote to him that

'...the directors of the Great Western Railway are desirous of obtaining your assistance in coming to a sound and practical conclusion as to their future proceedings.'

He was asked 'especially' to examine the 'peculiar' features of the Great Western compared with other railways, and his 182-page report in response deals with every facet of the construction of a railway. Wood did the survey requested, partly by visiting the works on the line, and partly by conducting experiments, the cost of which he subsequently charged to the Board. The advantage of experiments, he told the directors, was that his results would not be founded 'on mere opinion alone'.

On the question of the gauge, he concurred with Brunel that the reason for such a departure from the common gauge was the attainment of a higher rate of speed, that carriages were steadier and more roomy, and locomotives more powerful because of their greater size.

Above The broad gauge locomotive *North Star*, which was recorded as drawing 180 tons from London to Maidenhead at an average speed of nearly 38 miles per hour. *GWR Museum, Swindon*

Below North Star again, contrasted with later GWR locomotives at the same scale. The illustration is taken from the 1935 centenary issue of the *GWR Magazine*, at a time when the 'King' Class locomotives were able to take full advantage of the line that Brunel had so effectively laid out a century before. *GWR Museum, Swindon*

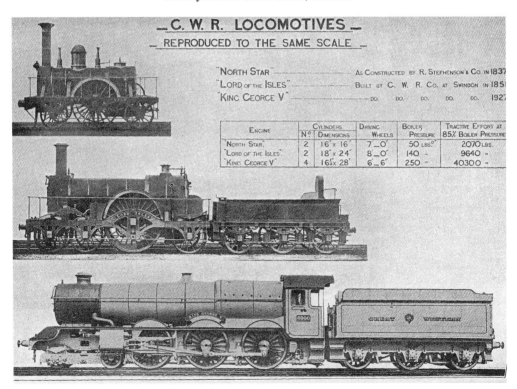

_ C. W. R. LOCOMOTIVES _
_ REPRODUCED TO THE SAME SCALE _

"NORTH STAR" —————— AS CONSTRUCTED BY R. STEPHENSON & Co. IN 1837
"LORD OF THE ISLES" —————— BUILT BY C. W. R. Co. AT SWINDON IN 1851
"KING GEORGE V" —————— DO. DO. DO. DO. DO. 1927

ENGINE	CYLINDERS		DRIVING	BOILER	TRACTIVE EFFORT AT
	N°.	DIMENSIONS	WHEELS	PRESSURE	85% BOILER PRESSURE
"NORTH STAR"	2	16" x 16"	7'_0"	50 LBS?	2070 LBS.
"LORD OF THE ISLES"	2	18" x 24"	8'_0"	140 "	9640 "
"KING GEORGE V"	4	16½" x 28"	6'_6"	250 "	40300 "

Having acknowledged that, Wood then asked if the increased speed achieved was worth the increased cost, and he recorded fuel consumption, speed and the loads drawn. He observed that *North Star* achieved an average performance from London to Maidenhead drawing 180 tons of nearly 38 miles per hour, with a top speed of 45mph on occasion. He observed that 'indisputable data' did not exist for other railway companies.

The issue of speed was of serious concern to the disbelieving attitudes of Members of Parliament founded in the 18th century; on the Liverpool & Manchester Committee in 1826 the promoters of the Bill were asked if they had had 'any doubt that a locomotive engine could be made to take the weight of forty tons at the rate of 6 miles an hour with perfect safety,' and they replied, 'An engine may go 6 miles an hour with forty tons.'

Wood was quite clear on the purposes of his experiments:

'It is admitted that the construction of that railway involves an increased capital; it is therefore quite necessary to determine what are the additional advantages in a practical point of view ... and whether the advantages are greater or less than are equivalent to the increased cost of construction.'

Sir John Hawkshaw was also asked about Brunel's engineering, and on 4 October 1838 he sent his report to the Great Western's directors. Like Wood, he had gone over the whole line, 'because on coming first upon your road that which immediately strikes is the large capacity of all things, engine, carriages and road, and the existence of such an arrangement presupposes, in my view, an equally large traffic.'

Sir John came to the conclusion, after a report of some 30 printed pages,

'...that there are no advantages to be obtained by adopting [the broad gauge] at all commensurate with the evils that will be consequent on the deviation; and ... it is not desirable ... to proceed with it'.

He was, of course, tied to the 'narrow' gauge lobby, and one might question how impartial his examination of Brunel's schemes had been. Sir John could not 'conceive that there is a single practical man in England who can recommend the 7 feet gauge as a general system for this country'. He argued that if it was not fit for the whole country, it would not be fit for a part of it. He warned the directors that even if the broad gauge were regarded as propitious for the Great Western, it could not be for the whole country.

He went on to tell the directors that their line presented good opportunities for investment, but 'its future prospects would depend ... upon the course you pursue... That course ... is not to go forward on your present system.'

Brunel responded to Sir John's and Wood's points in a letter to his directors dated 13 December 1838. Not for the first time, his exasperation with continually having to defend his system boiled over. He expressed his

'...regret at the manner in which the important questions at issue have been treated in the report [of Hawkshaw, which] has of itself prevented the discussion leading to any very satisfactory or useful conclusion. It has been almost impossible to do more than to show that whatever may be the state of the case, the views taken in the report and the arguments advanced are incorrect, and prove nothing.'

Wood then wrote to the directors, on 18 December. His letter came to some 80 printed pages, and covered every aspect of the development of early railways. He concluded that the additional expense of the broad gauge was not warranted by results, although he acknowledged that it did have some 'incidental' advantages. He added that the more widespread existence of the 'narrow' gauge meant the expense of a national conversion to broad gauge could not be justified. Brunel had received Wood's report on the 17th, and he soon wrote to his directors to tell them his opinion of it.

Brunel was confident of the ultimate outcome of his examination of the lengthy report, and spent four pages in a detailed rebuttal of Wood's experiments, on width, friction and track, and questioned the accuracy of some of his measuring experiments. The Great Western paid £3,200 for the experiments.

The report duly therefore came up for discussion at the proprietors' meeting. According to the report of the meeting in the *Bristol Mercury*, Heyworth said that

'…the errors into which Brunel had fallen were not trifling for, according to … [Heyworth's] opinion, it had taken out of his pocket [Heyworth's] no less than £70,000… [He concluded] that it would be much better to suspend the laying of the rails on the wide gauge.'

The company's Sealed Register records that despite Heyworth's claim of a £70,000 loss, he only had 25 shares (£2,500). By contrast, another Liverpool proprietor, a merchant called Nicholas Roskell, was impressed enough by the company to buy a total of 114 shares on several different occasions. In all, 34 Liverpool proprietors invested over £1,000 each.

Gibbs records in his diary the efforts he made to secure proxy votes against the amendment. He praises the 'admirable speech' of Samuel Gurney, a man who had invested £3,000 in the Stockton & Darlington in 1818. He had told the meeting on 9 January 1839 that speed was the object of all railways, and he believed – a belief confirmed by figures set out in the report of the Gauge Commissioners in 1846 – that greater speeds could be attained on the broad than on the narrow gauge. Gibbs went on to allude to how 'the wretched display made by our opponents combined to secure a complete triumph'. The extent to which the opposition to Brunel, as well as his support, were organised phenomena can be evidenced from the fact that 11,777 proxy votes were cast, 5,969 for the amendment, 5,908 against (one vote for each full share held, and proportionate votes for half- and fifth-shares). Those present at the meeting divided, however, more strongly in favour of Brunel; the result of the voting was that 225 proprietors at the meeting supported him and 135 voted against. His supporters held 5,831 shares, totalling 3,495 votes (again, one vote for each full share, and proportionate votes for half- and fifth-shares). His opponents held 2,650 shares, with 2,650 votes. Brunel's biographer Adrian Vaughan concludes that 'for better or worse, the Great Western was committed to the broad gauge and to Isambard Kingdom Brunel'. Chapter 1 has shown that this commitment to Brunel produced a top-quality railway and one that was very profitable for investors.

11.
RAILWAY DEVELOPMENT AND DAILY LIFE

'Whether we are wise to adopt the Great Western's speed is very doubtful. There is a
point to which the speed may be carried which becomes dangerous.'

George Hudson, 1846

This book has reviewed the processes involved in the railway revolution, illustrated throughout by the foundation of Isambard Kingdom Brunel's Great Western Railway. This railway revolution transformed people's daily lives, particularly in the developing urban centres of Great Britain. Fresh food became available because of the speed with which it could be transported across the country. A further consequence was the greater speed of communication offered by railways, along rails rather than difficult turnpike roads, and without cruelty to animals; moreover, rail travel was faster and more secure than coach travel had been formerly. Something of the tension this process generated, between the old world and the new, was, as one would expect, captured in another of Charles Saunders's cartoons, reproduced here.

THE SCALE OF RAILWAY DEVELOPMENT

The most obvious basis for the demand for railways was the escalation of trade caused by the expansion of the population and industrial production in the period during which railways were being established. Llewellyn Woodward draws attention to the fact that the population of England

New world meets old: 'Lady Baring's servant trying to recover his hat', a cartoon by Charles Saunders, c1840.
National Railway Museum, York

grew from 12,000,000 in 1811 to more than 21,000,000 in 1851. He attributes this principally to a decrease in infant mortality, but for the purposes of the present study it is important in demonstrating that the market for passenger traffic was expanding markedly during the period under consideration, and industrial production was also growing. The quantity of cotton goods manufactured in Great Britain grew from 92,525,951 pounds in 1815 to 354,196,602 in 1844, an increase of 383 per cent. This expansion of production fuelled the development of railways, and in turn the development of railways fuelled the expansion of production.

Dr Reed (1975) gives figures for the extent of railway development in the 1830s. He records that there were, between 1820 and 1839 inclusive, 186 Petitions to incorporate railways; 59 to extend the powers granted to railway companies; and 82 to grant railways further powers (45 in the years 1837-9 alone). These projects produced substantial profits for the proprietors – between January 1830 and June 1840 there was a growth of 172 per cent in railway share prices.

It was the prospect of capital and income profit that drove this 'Railway Mania' – there was little money to be made in the markets. Bank interest was 5 per cent or less, although there was no inflation. Railway capital was therefore attractive to investors, and between 1842 and 1846 it grew 145 per cent. Of course, the attraction of railways to investors had been demonstrated well before the incorporation of the Great Western Railway. By 1835 Stockton & Darlington shares had appreciated from an original price of £116 to £297; Liverpool & Manchester shares had appreciated by 210 per cent. There was also a prospect of a very quick return on capital – in 1836 York & North Midland £50 shares were selling at £54 when only £1 had been called up.

Net revenue grew by 178 per cent, boosting dividends as well as capital. The Great Western paid 3 to 4 per cent per half-year to 1846. However, this was miserly compared to the Liverpool & Manchester, which paid 10 per cent per half-year from 1841 to 1846. Equally, the London & Birmingham in the period 1837 to 1845 paid dividends ranging from 7 to 10 per cent for each half-year. Nevertheless, by the second half of 1848 the Great Western was turning in a surplus of more than £340,000 on receipts of £548,000, a very satisfactory gross profit.

Table 22 highlights the concerns that were to be expressed in Britain over the totally uncontrolled development of railways, which forms one of the main themes of this book. It shows that railway companies were turning in very substantial gross profits, ranging from more than a third to a half of receipts. While it covers a period extending two years beyond that of this book, it maps out clearly the basic trends in the development of railways in the 1830s. The ratio of expenditure to receipts for all these companies, the largest in Great Britain, demonstrates clearly what a profitable business railways were for their investors.

Many aspects of everyday life in Great Britain were transformed by the development of railways, and are examined in this chapter. First, there was the abovementioned new availability of fresh food in urban centres, essential to the transformation of the country from a predominantly agricultural economy to an industrial one. Second, there was the introduction of 'railway time', which meant that the whole country, for the first time, operated under a single time. Greater speeds of communication were engendered by the railway revolution, all previous modes being totally eclipsed by the speeds possible on rail, and last, the concept of class took hold – the type of people travelling 1st Class came to be described as 'the upper classes' and the others as the 'lower classes'.

An authoritative account of this is given by Professor Simmons in his book *The Victorian Railway*. When Samuel Laing was asked regarding the question of 3rd Class passengers being conveyed more cheaply, 'Are you aware whether there has been a pretty general clamour against third class passengers being conveyed in goods trains?' he replied that he was. He was then asked if he felt there was any real ground for that clamour. He said there was not, and that

Company	Miles open	Share\loan capital	Expenditure as a % of receipts	Dividend
Great Western	81.75	£6,651,900	41%	6%
Eastern Counties	117.50	£2,737,000	51%	1.25%
Grand Junction	101.50	£2,375,000	44%	10%
London & Birmingham	112.00	£4,237,500	33%	10%
London & South Western	92.75	£2,585,700	45%	5.5%
Midland Counties	57.00	£1,725,600	59%	3%
North Midland	73.75	£3,340,000	40%	3.25%
South Eastern	47.00	£2,530,000	n/a	n/a

Table 22: Receipts, expenditure and return on capital of the principal railways, 1842

it had arisen 'when it was apprehended that there was more danger from travelling in goods trains', and that 3rd Class travel was therefore not perceived as being more dangerous than 1st or 2nd Class travel. While his evidence shows concerns at the concept of cheap-fare-paying – and hence largely poorer – members of society being treated like animals, it nevertheless shows that such a poor standard of rail travel was acceptable to early Victorian society.

DAILY LIFE TRANSFORMED

Consumption of fresh food

In the Commons the Earl of Kerry, Member of Parliament for Calne in Wiltshire, drew attention to the Great Western's 'national importance, for by it the best and most wholesome food would be obtained by the labouring classes of this great metropolis more cheaply'.

To demonstrate demand for railways, local traders were commonly brought before Select Committees by the promoters of railways. In the Great Western's case in 1835, a fishmonger from Bristol spoke in support of the line, and set out the problems he faced in Bristol in getting his stock from London in reasonable condition: roads were bad, and he suffered from pilferage on river transportation. He subsequently showed his support for the Great Western by buying five shares.

Equally, the evidence given to the House of Lords Committee on the Great Western in 1835 by John G. Lamb, a tallow chandler from Reading, may be reasonably cited as typical of the reaction of trade to the coming of the railways. He told the Committee that the railway 'would very much increase the trade of Reading ... and there is a feeling in Reading in favour of the railway.' The advantages to his line of business were speed, cost and reliability. He used Russian tallow, which he bought in London in quantities of 20 to 50 casks at a time. He paid 6s 9d per cask, then brought it to Reading by water. The cost of carriage was 9d per cask by water, and 1s 9d per cask by road, although he never used road transport because of pilferage, and he was 'frequently' inconvenienced by delay. He also sold Irish butter, which suffered equally from delay in carriage. He felt that he had to buy it from London rather than Bristol, but would have preferred to buy it in Bristol, from where he thought it could be bought 'fresh and cheap'. This witness subsequently bought five shares in the Great Western undertaking, at a cost of £500.

The Great Western arranged for various local Bristol businessmen to give evidence to the Commons Committee in 1834, and they supported the Great Western's assertion that the route would be of advantage to commerce in Bristol. A Bristol tea-dealer told the Committee that 'he had conveyed his goods from Bristol to London by the Kennet & Avon Canal and had been very frequently inconvenienced by delay.' In 1826 'he had started to send goods by land, which he had found a more expensive mode in consequence of the danger and delay.' Robert Cordwent, a farmer, told the Commons Select Committee, referring to the journey from Bristol to London, that 'sometimes it would extend into a fortnight or three weeks'.

Other railway companies also produced before their Select Committees local tradesmen to support their undertakings. Thus the London & Birmingham Railway produced as a witness on 29 June 1832 Harman Earle, a Liverpool merchant who was also a director of the railway. Equally, the witnesses for the York & North Midland in 1836, in addition to engineers and surveyors, included John Wilkinson, a nurseryman; John Brutton, a linen and carpet manufacturer; George Craddock, a rope manufacturer; and Charles Hansen, a druggist from York. George Hudson himself was a carpet trader in York as well as being the main promoter of the York company.

It was the view of the Reading *Mercury* that food supplies to London would be improved by the Great Western, employment would be created, and property prices in Reading would rise. Certainly, the employed population in the three Reading parishes, St Giles, St Lawrence and St Mary, grew from 21,238 in 1831 to 24,717 in 1841.

The coming of the railways also improved diet in Britain. One of the projected advantages of the greater speed offered by railways was that they would make fresh food available to all classes of society in the big, recently industrialised cities. Details of the increases in the consumption of fish, which had occurred in the aftermath of the coming of the railways, were set out by Samuel Salt in 1848. He states that in 1829 there were ten fish merchants in Birmingham, but that that number had grown since the opening of the railway to 40 in the city itself, with additional uncounted merchants 'in the suburbs'. Table 23 sets out the increase in the quantities of fish being consumed over the whole country; in the ten years from the opening of the Liverpool & Manchester, the average consumption of fish increased, as a result of the coming of the railways, by almost five times.

An increase was also recorded in the sales of cattle and sheep at London's Smithfield Market: 159,907 cattle and 1,287,070 sheep were sold in 1830, but the figure for cattle increased to 177,497 in 1840, and that for sheep to 1,371,370. Equally, railways fuelled the expansion of industry. The tonnage of coal brought to London grew from 2,116,023 in 1830 to 2,589,087 in 1840.

Railways were a significant factor in the decline of fresh food prices. George Porter uses the weekly book of St Thomas's Hospital in Southwark to give statistics for the cost of beef and lamb purchased, which are 'strictly comparative'. His figures show that the price of beef, per stone, was 4s 4d in 1825 and in 1842 had fallen to 3s 4d. Over the period 1825 to 1845 the value of £1,000 had deflated, from £45,737 at 1997 prices to £45,300. In real terms, therefore, food was becoming significantly cheaper during the railway revolution. While factors other than railways clearly played their role in this process, the readier availability to markets offered to producers by the new speed of communication was of great importance.

Year	Tons of fish consumed	Tons per head of population (% change)
1829	400	0.003 (100)
1834	1,500	0.009 (300)
1840	2,500	0.014 (467)

Table 23: The growth in fish consumption

'Railway time'

Arguably the most widespread change in British society resulting from the introduction of railways was that of standard time over the whole of Great Britain. Until the 1780s the different times that existed as one travelled between west and east had been uncomplainingly accepted. There was almost half an hour's difference between Penzance and Yarmouth. However, the opening of railways and the speed of communication they gave quickly led to dissatisfaction with local times. The Liverpool & Manchester Railway therefore petitioned Parliament to legislate to abolish local time in 1845, and the Railway Clearing House passed a resolution recommending all its members to adhere to London time, but some local opposition remained. The Royal Observatory formed a partnership with the South Eastern Railway to transmit its time signals by a specially laid telegraph line, which was brought into use in 1852. However, the Great Western had already adopted London time in 1840, and this came to be known as 'railway time'.

GREAT WESTERN RAILWAY.—The public are informed that this RAILWAY will be OPENED for the CONVEYANCE of PASSENGERS only between London, West Drayton, Slough, and Maidenhead station, on Monday, the 4th June. The following will be the times for the departure of trains each way, from London and from Maidenhead, (excepting on Sundays,) until further notice:—

Trains each way.

8 o'clock morning	;	4 o'clock afternoon.
9 o'clock ditto		5 o'clock ditto
10 o'clock ditto		6 o'clock ditto
12 o'clock noon		7 o'clock ditto

Trains on Sundays each way.

7 o'clock morning	;	5 o'clock afternoon.
8 o'clock ditto		6 o'clock ditto
9 o'clock ditto		7 o'clock ditto

Each train will take up or set down passengers at West Drayton and Slough.

Fares of Passengers.

	First Class.		Second Class.	
	Posting Carriage.	Passenger Coach.	Coach.	Open Carriage.
	s. d.	s. d.	s. d.	s. d.
Paddington Station to West Drayton	4 0	3 6	2 0	1 6
to Slough	5 6	4 6	3 0	2 6
to Maidenhead	6 6	5 6	4 0	3 6

Notice is also given that on and after Monday, the 11th June, carriages and horses will be conveyed on the railway, and passengers and parcels booked for conveyance by coaches in connexion with the Railway Company to the west of England, including Stroud, Cheltenham, and Glocester, as well as to Oxford, Reading, Henley, Marlow, Windsor, Uxbridge, and other contiguous places. By order of the Directors,
CHARLES A. SAUNDERS, } Secs.
THOMAS OSLER,

The Great Western Railway's first timetable shows departure but not arrival times in the years before 'railway time' was adopted.
GWR Museum, Swindon

Stage coaches advertised the length of time their journeys would take, but not their arrival times. For a period this was also true of railways, as can be seen from the Great Western's first timetable reproduced here. 'Railway time' was subsequently brought in, then in 1840 Greenwich Mean Time brought the whole country on to a single time scale.

Railways also drew the nation together in other ways: circulation figures for *The Times* newspaper show that railways enabled news to be disseminated from London to the regions far more effectually than had ever been the case before. The circulation of *The Times* was 11,000 on 26 June 1830, the death of King George IV, and on 11 February 1839, the date of Queen Victoria's betrothal to Albert, had increased to 30,000. Stanley Baldwin, three times Prime Minister, stated that, 'I doubt if historians have done full justice to the makers of railways as the makers of nations.'

Speed of communication

A significant effect on British society was the speed of communication provided by railways. The backcloth against which this transformation was experienced was the speed of road, river and canal transport, and its consequence was the increased use of transport. Professor Simmons has estimated (1986) that in the 1830s the number of passengers conveyed daily by public transport in Great Britain was 220,000. The Bristol Committee set up to promote the Great Western assumed that only a doubling of the numbers of passengers carried on the route in stage-coaches would be achieved. William Shearman, of the Stage Coach Department of the Stamp Office, told the House of Commons Committee on the Great Western Bill in 1834 that a total of 188 journeys were being made by 13 coaches from Bath to Bristol, and William Sutherland, of the same Office, told the Committee that 136 journeys were being made along various sections of the route between London and Bristol weekly by 20 coaches. The 1833 prospectus drew attention to the number of 'much-frequented' towns on the route that would generate passenger demand for the railway. Promoters of other railways were similarly asked by their Parliamentary Committees about the predicted traffic and invariably gave figures for stage-coach travel on the proposed routes.

In fact, in the Great Western's case, as well as that of other railways, a much higher increase in the levels of travel was achieved. The Great Western line opened to Maidenhead in the second half of 1838 and carried 359,076 passengers from then to the end of 1838. Figures for the following years show Brunel's estimates had been by no means optimistic, and passenger figures increased to a level of 1,441,255 in 1845. Equally, the surplus of income over expenditure increased from £157,678 in the first half of 1842 to £293,690 in the second half of 1845.

The extent and nature of the transformation in Great Britain to be introduced by the railways in the 1830s was set out in the prospectus of the London & Birmingham Railway, incorporated in 1833. This stated that

'... above all, the public must derive a benefit which cannot easily be estimated from the power the railway will give for the rapid transmission of intelligence, bullion, troops and military stores, in connection with the steam boats; it will reduce the time of passing between London and Dublin within four and twenty hours.'

The speeds of different railways are set out in Table 24, drawn from Bradshaw's timetables for 1841.

An impression of the arguments in favour of the broad gauge from the point of view of speed can be obtained from Brunel's own words, when he explained to the Gauge Commissioners on 25 October 1845 why he had decided that the broad gauge was superior:

'Looking to the speeds which I contemplated would be adopted on railways, and the masses to be moved, it seemed to me that the whole machine was too small for the work to be done, and that it required that the parts should be on a scale more commensurate with the mass and velocity to be attained.'

However, when George Hudson appeared before the Commissioners, he unashamedly appealed to the traditionalists on the Commission:

Journey	Distance (miles)	Fastest service	Speed (mph)
Great Western (London to Bristol)	118	4hr 23min	26.8
London & Birmingham			
(London to Birmingham)	112.5	5hr 15min	21.4
Manchester & Birmingham			
(Manchester to Birmingham)	78	4hr 20min	18.1
Midland Railway (London to Derby)	88	6hr 30min	13.5
London, Brighton & South Coast Railway			
(London to Brighton)	50	2hr 0min	25.0

Table 24: Speeds on Great Britain's principal railways

'A family applying Wray's aromatic spice powder': Saunders's cartoon (c1840) depicts a family applying the powder preparatory to undertaking a railway journey; mother applies some patent remedy to one of her children, presumably as protection against the rigours of rail travel, while her husband reads the manufacturer's leaflet. *National Railway Museum, York*

'I am not aware that we are not competent to attain the speed of the Great Western. Whether we are wise to adopt that speed is very doubtful. There is a point to which the speed may be carried which becomes dangerous.'

Brunel had to answer patiently in 1846 to the Gauge Commissioners' very old-fashioned fears of railways. The Saunders cartoon here reproduced mirrors that fear. Brunel was asked if the speed he had given express trains was more dangerous for the public than speeds before had been. Brunel replied that there was not much difference. He acknowledged that 60 miles per hour did involve some 'increased danger' compared to travelling at 40 miles per hour, but said that the increased danger was met by 'increased precautions'. All things considered, 'the express trains are as safe as the others'.

Travel in different classes

A further major change in Great Britain resulting at least in part from the railway development process in the 1830s was the emergence of class consciousness. Formerly, stage-coach travel had been divided into classes based upon the quality of transport: inside, outside or wagon travel. Railways divided passengers, not just the trains themselves, into five distinct classes, resulting ultimately in 1st, 2nd and 3rd Class travellers. This began with the Liverpool & Manchester Railway, which adopted classes at first only to describe trains (that is, quick or slow), but in 1837 the Grand Junction Railway first spoke of 1st and 2nd Class passengers.

However, railways also had the effect of levelling rather than reinforcing class distinctions: a Lord who had formerly travelled in his own coach now found himself travelling alongside any paying passenger, which brought him into contact with other classes of people. Thus the journalist Samuel Sydney portrayed a dignified peer, who would formerly have travelled in his own carriage, sharing a 1st Class compartment at Euston with the travelling representative of a wine merchant and a newspaper reporter. In the past no one of rank had ever travelled in a public coach in the company of strangers.

The report of Samuel Laing to the 1844 Select Committee on Railways, from whose recommendations sprang Gladstone's 'Parliamentary mile' of the 1844 Railways Act, observed that the total number of passengers in each class in 1842 had been as shown in Table 25. The most marked feature is the relatively small percentage of passengers on the Great Western Railway who travelled 3rd Class compared to the percentage for the whole country.

Laing's report excluded the Great Western from a listing of railways that had 'adopted the Third-Class System fully' or to 'a considerable extent', then listed seven companies that 'reject or limit the third class system'. These were the Grand Junction, the Great Western, the London & Birmingham, the London & South Western, the Liverpool & Manchester, the North Union, and the Newcastle & Carlisle.

The Committee cited the details set out in Table 26, showing average fares per mile in 1842. By this date the Great Western had absorbed the Cheltenham & Great Western and the Bristol & Exeter railways, hence their absence from the table in their own right.

Laing was then asked if he believed 'that if it was left open to companies to run third-class carriages with goods trains, that would be a means of checking the invasion of the second-class traffic?' He replied that he thought it would. Nevertheless, some companies ran trains without carriages for 3rd Class passengers, and it was not until the Midland Railway decided to make all its services available to all classes in 1872 that the other companies followed suit. Apart from Denmark, no European country went so far before 1914.

This chapter, then, has illustrated the transformation of life in Great Britain consequent upon railway development. It does not presume to match Professor Simmons's wide-ranging and authoritative review of this transformation in *The Victorian Railway*, but has sought to complement that work.

	1st Class	2nd Class	3rd Class
Total number	3,686,022	9,204,654	7,121,605
Percentage, all railways	18.4%	46%	35.6%
Percentage, Great Western	25.1%	67.2%	7.6%

Table 25: Passenger figures in different classes, 1842

Railway	1st Class	2nd Class	3rd Class
Eastern Counties	2.65	1.87	1.46
Great Western	3.031	2.085	1.183
Liverpool & Manchester	2.4	1.77	n/a
London & Birmingham	3.214	2.143	1.5
London & Brighton	3.5	2.25	1.5
London & South Western	3.1	2.12	1.2
Manchester & Birmingham	3	2.33	1.25
Manchester & Leeds	3	2	1
Midland Counties	3	2	1
North Midland	3	2	1.5
South Eastern	2.33	1.64	0.86

Table 26: Average fare per mile on the principal British railways, 1842 (old pence)

12.

CONCLUSION: THE PLACE OF BRUNEL'S GREAT WESTERN IN RAILWAY INCORPORATION IN THE 1830s

'The evidence has most satisfactorily established the importance of this line of communication and the correctness of the calculations of revenue, as well as the sufficiency of the estimates of cost.'

Great Western directors, 2 September 1834

Railway incorporation was a marked feature of political life in the 1830s. The 1839 Select Committee on Railways reported that in the years 1836 to 1839 £41,618,014 of capital had been authorised, and £16,177,630 in loan-raising powers; the equivalent figure today is almost £2.5 billion. These quantities were a wholly new phenomenon in Great Britain, and led to discussion of whether and how public control should be established, the most marked such contemporary assessment being that of the 1839 Select Committee on Railways.

PUBLIC CONTROL

It is obvious that the introduction of any element of public control of railways in the 1830s presupposed the active involvement of civil servants. Therefore the evidence to the 1844 Select Committee on Railways of Samuel Laing, the head of the Railways Department of the Board of Trade, which had been established in 1840, is of great, albeit retrospective, significance.

Laing's views give a personal slant to public policy on the control of the new railway network and the scale of its expansion. He answered 1,989 questions, principally on the Government's perception of the development of railways. His views go some way to explain why, in Britain, railway development took place with virtually no public control.

Nevertheless, there was some involvement of the executive Government in the regulation of railways by Parliament. In this period Select Committees were not as independent of the Government as they are today: the 1844 Select Committee on Railways was chaired by Gladstone, who was then President of the Board of Trade and therefore had executive responsibility for the Government's role in the overseeing of railways. In addition, Select Committees were used by Government to air public discussion of issues, and Government legislated immediately after the Committees had reported. Thus Gladstone's Committee's report led directly to the Railways Act of 1844; in the same way, the Gauge Commission's report in 1846, recommending that all railways in future be authorised only on the 'narrow' gauge, received the sanction of Parliament only days after it had been presented to Parliament.

The Board of Trade's Samuel Laing told the Committee that his Department's role in the regulation of railways was almost entirely limited to regulations concerning public safety, a subject depicted with grim humour in the frontispiece to Charles Saunders's collection of cartoons (c1840). *National Railway Museum, York*

Laing told the Committee that his Department's role in the regulation of railways was almost entirely limited to regulations regarding public safety. He was asked why the Government did not take a proactive role in the development of railways, and he replied that it had been

'...very much from the practical difficulty of dealing with the great number of railway Bills that were brought before Parliament in the years 1836 and 1837, and the very protracted and difficult nature of the inquiries; and it was felt that to have undertaken that sort of supervision, at that period, when so little was known about the principles which were to regulate railway legislation, might have converted the Board of Trade, in fact, into a tribunal for doing nothing else than attending to railway Bills pending during the Session.'

His concern was founded upon the fact that in 1836 and 1837 there were 77 Bills relating to railways, some for new companies (44) and the rest to amend the powers of already existing companies. Laing told the Committee that some discretionary power should 'definitely' be vested in a public department, but that that department should 'certainly' *not* be the Board of Trade. Some impression of why Laing was so worried can be gauged from the fact that despite the flurry of railway incorporation Bills in the 1830s, in 1844 his department still had only five staff (the whole Board had 30 staff at this time).

A further aspect of the manner in which railway development was considered by both Government and the Houses of Parliament was Standing Order No 33 of the House of Commons. This required a deposit of 10 per cent of the capital before a Bill could be proceeded with, and Laing suggested that figure be reduced to 5 per cent, as required in the House of

Lords. He believed that the advantage would be to encourage 'legitimate railway enterprise', as the current 10 per cent figure was an obstacle to true railway development, and encouraged profiteering. He was concerned at the number of companies being set up as satellites of the big companies, such as the Great Western, and he told the Committee that a reduced deposit would lead to more independent companies. This would stop the establishment of what Laing described as 'bubble' companies. The Committee discussed Laing's point with him at considerable length, and he cited as an example the Northampton & Peterborough line, which had been sponsored by the London & Birmingham. Laing concluded that it

'...would be possible to make that reduction without danger of encouraging that which it was the wish to repress by requiring a deposit of ten per cent.'

The extent to which Government was becoming involved in the regulation of railways was set out by Laing when he gave evidence to the Select Committee on Railway Bills on 7 February 1845. He told it that in that Session 108 schemes for railways had been submitted, on all of which the Board of Trade had had to report. The Railway Board had reported in favour of 47, against 45, and recommended the postponement of 16. Laing's evidence therefore illustrated that Government was, at that stage, unready to assume the more interventionist State role to protect individuals that it had to assume as the Industrial Revolution progressed. Other evidence given by Laing confirmed his horror at the prospect of becoming responsible for the vast and growing numbers of railway Bills. He discussed the question of public and private interests, and referred to the question of the Board of Trade regulating private property.

'When you are interfering ... with private property in order to obtain an important public line of railway, an isolated case may arise where a very small amount of opposition might defeat the whole thing; in that case I should certainly prefer leaving it to the Board of Trade. I look upon it as something like the dispensing power which we have of authorising railway companies to take land not included in their Act of Parliament, when rendered necessary for the prevention of accidents.'

Laing was referring to the problems caused by a Standing Order limiting the power of railway companies to deviate even by a few feet from their authorised line:

'There have certainly been cases where railways have been very nearly stopped in their construction altogether by this Standing Order, and others have only escaped by paying what the landowners asked for the land.'

Clearly, then, Government was far from ready to assume responsibility for the public benefit and was still relieved to let the issues raised by railway speculation be settled by market forces and Parliamentary scrutiny.

Laing came under question on the balance of 'public good' against 'private interests':

'Supposing you were the only persons to determine the question, assuming this power to be given, you would consider the general public convenience, through the medium of cheap fares, and so forth, rather than the rights of property, or the disposition of individuals to live in a particular place, and which would be interfered with by the construction of the railway in a particular manner?'

Laing replied:

> 'If the Bill had been sanctioned by Parliament upon the ground of public utility, there
> would be a *prima facie* presumption in favour of such improvement to the public at
> the expense of a comparatively small private right.'

Laing later went on to talk of the difficulties that railway promoters experienced in getting a
fair price fixed for property. He was asked if he had 'ever heard of any very striking instance of
an outrageous price being demanded as the condition of consent to the passing of the Bill', and
replied, 'Yes, I have heard it stated generally.' He gave as an example the Great North of
England Railway

> '...where there had been some slight alteration in a bridge crossing the railway. The
> parties had petitioned, and they had obliged the railway company to expense –
> altogether £4,000 or £5,000 – to make this bridge for the road to cross the railway; and
> then, on account of some slight non-compliance with the requisition of the Act, which
> General Paisley, who had looked at the place for the Board of Trade, reported as a
> decided improvement, they are bringing actions against the railway company for
> depriving them of the right of level crossing. They are insisting upon having both the
> original right of level crossing and the right of using the diverted road over the bridge.'

Thus Laing's evidence is of importance in giving a personal slant that goes some way towards
explaining the 'hands-off' attitude of the British Government to the new railway companies in
the 1830s. However, his Minister at the Board of Trade in 1844 was Gladstone, and he was to play
an important role in establishing some Government control. While this originated with
Gladstone himself, the evidence Laing gave to the 1844 Select Committee on Railways
demonstrates that Gladstone certainly did not encounter any opposition from his civil servants.

EXPANSION AND PROFITABILITY

Despite all Britain's principal railways having been authorised by 1840, the network was still
expanding at the end of the 1840s, with 9,979 miles being authorised between 1844 and 1848,
at a total capital cost of £195,438,666. Additionally, loan-raising powers were £70,369,873 over
the years 1844 to 1848. The rates of dividends were, however, good. Over the period 1842 to
1846 average dividends peaked at 5 per cent, with a low of 3.2 per cent in 1846. As has been
observed, this was in a period with no inflation.

Two of the most important railways that here provide the framework for the assessment
of the role of the State in the development of Great Britain's railways are the Great Western and
the London & Birmingham. A comparison of the relative costs of each was given in an appendix
to the report of the Gauge Commissioners in 1846, giving figures for the two years to 30 June
1845 for both companies. They received broadly the same level of receipts: the Great Western
£1,617,995 compared to the London & Birmingham's £1,735,796. Total mileage for passengers
was also broadly the same: the Great Western recorded 128,524,232, the London & Birmingham
121,529,606. However, Great Western trains were much less crowded. While passenger mileage
was broadly similar, the distance travelled by the Great Western's trains was about a quarter
more than on the London & Birmingham, at an average number of passengers per train of 47.2
compared to 84.9. However, the Saunders cartoon reproduced here displays a contempt

'Sale of the Effects of the Sufferer on the Railway': this Saunders cartoon (c1840) depicts an auction of a dead man's possessions, perhaps some poor passenger who died in a rail accident. *National Railway Museum, York*

towards passengers somewhat inappropriate for the servant of a railway that drew the vast bulk of its income from passengers.

The Gauge Commissioners' report gives figures for the ratio of costs for the two railways in this period, and interesting differences emerge that confirm Brunel's assurances to his Board that the extra costs of his engineering proposals would be repaid. The most evident feature is that the Great Western cost more to equip yet was cheaper to travel on than the London & Birmingham. It is also evident that the cost of engine repairs was lower on the Great Western, perhaps as a result of Brunel having persuaded his Board to spend more on the initial capital cost of locomotives.

Cost was obviously a critical feature of Brunel's plans, which he estimated would come to £2,805,300, including engineering works, rolling-stock, and the cost of 'Parliamentary and other preliminary expenses'. Saunders was asked by the Parliamentary Committee on the Great Western Bill in 1835 to set out the particulars of the company's estimate for making the railway, and the details of his assessment were given above. It is of interest that the evidence for the Great Western's 1835 Committee includes no discussion of the gauge of the Great Western. Equally, it illustrates how important to the development of early railways the question of land compensation was: this question figures large in the Committee, as well as in other companies' evidence sessions. For example, the Secretary of the North Midland Railway was subjected to an intensive grilling on the extent of 'local' support for his railway, and this is of significance in demonstrating why railways came to focus the role of the State, and the conflict of the issues of 'public good' and 'private interests' of landowners. The Great Western therefore illustrates wider issues in the development of railways and of the State's role in society as the protector of 'private interests'. All these expenses obviously contributed to the cost of rail travel, but there was much concern, notably in Gladstone's 1844 Select Committee on Railways, at the manner in which these costs were being translated into fares. Certainly, the cost of rail travel in Great Britain was dramatically higher than elsewhere in Europe, as shown in Table 27.

The Committee then went on to set out the cost of the construction of Great Britain's railways. As already mentioned above, they found that these varied between about £9,000 per mile (the Dundee & Arbroath) and £59,800 (the Manchester & Leeds). The Great Western was the third most expensive, at £56,300 per mile, with the London & Birmingham at £53,100.

Country	1st Class	2nd Class	3rd Class
England	25s (100%)	17s (100%)	10s (100%)
Belgium	10s (50%)	7s 6d (44%)	4s 8d (47%)
France	15s (60%)	10s (59%)	6s 8d (66.6%)
Germany	12s (48%)	8s 6d (50%)	5s 6d (55%)

Table 27: Cost of rail travel per 100 miles, 1844

Railways in the United States cost an average of £4,800 per mile, but in France the cost of construction cited by the 1844 Committee ranged from £7,500 per mile for the Etienne & Andrizieux to £55,600 for the Paris & Versailles.

The profile of spending by the Great Western was different from that of other railway companies in that it was growing at so much greater a rate, and needed money to fund that process. Thus the Great Western's share capital grew from £2,500,000 in 1835 to £4,650,100 in 1840. Additionally, it had taken on the capital of the companies it had leased, such as the Cheltenham & Great Western Union (£750,000) and the Bristol & Exeter (£1,500,000). The Great Western's capital demands were substantial during the period of construction, but the company was also able to fund the purchase of the Oxford and Cheltenham & Great Western Union railways from the capital raised in 1839. It also paid for the lease of the Bristol & Exeter in 1840. The London & Birmingham was much less expansionist: its share and loan capital grew from £3,335,000 on incorporation in 1833 to £5,500,000 in 1840 (61 per cent) compared to a figure for the Great Western of 182 per cent. In the period 1835 to 1840, the Great Western issued 87,505 shares with an aggregate value of £4,500,100.

An impression of the relative weight attached to the costs of land and construction was given by Brunel in evidence to the House of Commons Committee on the Great Western (Paddington) Bill in 1837. The line proposed by that Bill was to be 4½ miles in length, linking Acton to Paddington, and thereby giving the Great Western its own station in London (it had formerly used the London & Birmingham's). Brunel told the Committee that the cost of construction would be £250,000, and the cost of land purchases £170,000. No extra capital would be required to be raised for the purposes of the Bill.

Brunel achieved a wholly deserved reputation for under-estimating the cost of his projects for the Great Western, but that railway was not by any means alone in this. It was accepted uncomplainingly by the 1839 Select Committee on Railways, which reported that

> '...there can be no doubt as to the accuracy of the statements made by several of the witnesses that it was impossible before the opening of the railroads to calculate the nature and extent of the accommodation which would be required to meet the convenience of the public; and thus the estimates presented to Parliament ... have been deficient to a very great extent.'

Some impression of why these over-runs on estimates were occurring was given to the Select Committee on Railways by Robert Stephenson. He told it, when he was asked about public accommodation being larger than his company had originally anticipated would be required, that

> '...at the time the estimate of the London & Birmingham Railway was made, it was apprehended that something like £2,500 or £3,000 for a station at each end of the line

was ample; but they have exceeded $10,000. I have no hesitation in saying that the expense of stations has been eight or ten-fold beyond that originally contemplated... The Liverpool & Manchester at that time was fitted up very much on that scale of station which cost $1,500 or $2,000; they have gone on increasing the accommodation to the public as necessity demanded; but when we made the estimate we were not prepared for those accommodations.'

Significantly, Robert Stephenson sought to make these excesses acceptable by setting them in the context of 'public needs' rather than an anticipated increase of profitability of the service offered.

REACTIONS TO BRUNEL

Alfred Pugsley (1976) refers to the importance of Brunel as a man who unusually bridged the separate fields of engineering: mechanical, civil, and electrical. The range and importance of his role in almost all aspects of the Great Western's foundation have been emphasised throughout this book, which has also brought out his involvement in the Great Western's development on the political stage, and how relatively unsuccessful that was.

One consequence of Brunel's supremacy over most aspects of the company's development was that in its earliest days the Great Western had no timetables. Saunders told the Parliamentary Committee on Railways in 1841:

'At the opening in 1838 we found the engines were so inefficient that time-table working was hopeless; one or two engines might keep time, the other 8 or 10 were always out of time. So we suspended time-tables till the locomotive power became sufficient.'

Robert Stephenson's company in Newcastle built 12 locomotives for the Great Western over the period November 1837 to November 1841, which had working lives ranging from 25 to 33 years. Jones, Turner & Evans of Newton in Lancashire built six engines for the company, all delivered in 1840, which had working lives ranging from 26 to 38 years. Firms delivering locomotives during the period under consideration were based in Manchester, Leeds, London and one firm in Bristol, Stobert & Slaughter, whose two engines lasted 23 and 29 years.

Despite its subsequent epithet as 'God's Wonderful Railway' on the grounds not least of its speed and the comfort of the accommodation offered to passengers, the early unreliability of engines on the Great

Charles Saunders (1796-1864), Secretary of the Great Western Railway. *GWR Museum, Swindon*

Western was a problem ultimately solved by the employment of Daniel Gooch as the Locomotive Superintendent at the end of July 1837, at the age of only 21 (Brunel had been 33 when appointed by the Bristol Committee). Gooch had worked with Robert Stephenson at the Vulcan Foundry in Northumberland and was later to become the Chairman of the Great Western from 1863 to 1889, the period Tim Bryan describes as the 'Golden Age' of the Great Western. The combination of Brunel's immense skills as a civil engineer and those of Gooch as a locomotive engineer went a considerable way towards making this railway 'wonderful'.

Two engines Brunel had built by Stephenson & Co in Newcastle were to drawings by Gooch, and he also designed an engine for Russia to a 6-foot gauge, which was remodelled to the 7-foot gauge, the celebrated *North Star*. Gooch was paid £300 a year (the modern equivalent is around £18,000). This sum increased to £550 on the opening of the first section of the line and to £1, 700 in January 1841, which showed how much the Great Western's directors recognised the value of his services, even if Brunel was irritated by the diminution of his own control.

The Great Western's official reaction to the defeat of 1834 came in a pamphlet sent to shareholders on 2 September 1834. The directors assured the proprietors of 'their exertions to carry it [the Bill] to a successful issue', and that their labours had been 'unremitting', although 'unavailing' during the Session. The document shows awareness of the root cause of the defeat, the 'divided route', which had been approved by one House of Parliament after 'a most searching and protracted investigation', alluding to the long Commons Committee stage. They observed that the Bill had been lost in the Lords largely because of the time

Sir Daniel Gooch in later life.
GWR Museum, Swindon

question, which 'would have been insufficient for another investigation before a Committee of the House of Lords'. The Directors undertook to publish a selection of the Commons proceedings, which would be forwarded to all proprietors to act 'as the justification of their proceedings'. They drew attention to the unprecedented perseverance shown by the opposition to the Bill, which demonstrated both 'the importance of the undertaking and the real merits of the case, which triumphed over every difficulty in the House of Commons, where alone they came under investigation'. The evidence the directors had placed before the Committee had conclusively demonstrated 'the importance of this line of communication and the correctness of the calculations of revenue, as well as the sufficiency of the estimates of cost'. They referred to the evidence of their 'most influential' Parliamentary supporters, and assured the proprietors that the proposal in the next Session of Parliament of a route from London all the way to Bristol would 'unquestionably receive the sanction of the legislature'. The Directors pointed out that a similar fate had befallen the Liverpool & Manchester, which had also been rejected on its first application to Parliament, and they considered it 'their duty' to raise sufficient subscriptions to enable them to put forward a Bill for the whole route next Session. That would, in any case, be in the best interests of proprietors who had invested in anticipation of the line being built. To this end, new shares would be created and offered initially to existing shareholders. The Directors urged shareholders to exercise this option, taking the new shares or selling them to friends.

Brunel reflected on this dramatic sequence of events in his diary entry for 26 December 1835:

> 'I had been toiling most unprofitably at numerous things… I am [now] engineer to the finest work in England – a handsome salary – £2,000 a year – on excellent terms with my directors and all going smoothly, but what a fight we have had – and how near defeat – and what a ruinous defeat it would have been. It is like looking back upon a fearful pass – but we have succeeded, and it's not this alone but everything I have been engaged in has been very successful.'

He then listed those successes: Clifton Bridge, Sunderland Docks, Bristol Docks, the Merthyr & Cardiff Railway, the Cheltenham Railway, the Bristol & Exeter Railway, the Newbury Branch, and the suspension bridge across the Thames. He concluded that, 'I think this forms a pretty list of real profitable, sound professional jobs – unsought for on my part, that is, given to me fairly by the respective parties.' This spirit of smugness permeated the man and the company he founded. When the Great Western was the only company to retain its identity under the Grouping of railways in 1923, this added fuel to this fire. The Great Western's company magazine issued the cartoon reproduced below to mark the escape that recalls the spirit of Isambard Kingdom Brunel most acutely.

A SURVIVAL OF TITLE.

DICK GERMAN

THE GREAT WESTERN: "Hooray! Never even blew me cap off!"

The Great Western retains its identity at the 1923 Grouping.
GWR Museum, Swindon

STATE INVESTMENT

The incorporation of the Great Western, because of the number of property owners affected by it and its effect upon two important political interests, Eton College and Oxford University, raised the question of the State's proper role in the development of Great Britain's railways. As we have already seen, this was a topic of great interest to William Galt, who wrote a pamphlet calling for *Railway Reform*, by which he meant taking railways into public ownership. This came out in the climate of Gladstone's 1844 Select Committee report on railways, which called for the same thing. Galt's views were sufficiently important for him to be called to give oral evidence to that Committee.

Galt gave the Select Committee an assessment of the current market value of railways in Great Britain. Table 28 extracts the data for the six principal railways, arranged in descending order of value, including the earliest passenger railway, the Liverpool & Manchester. The most striking feature of the table is how much more successful the London & Birmingham was than most of the other major companies in terms of the value of the company: its market value was 2.2 times its cost, and only the Liverpool & Manchester matched that figure. The Great Western's market value was only £12,000 more than its cost. The largest depreciation was shown by the Eastern Counties, which had a market value 0.84 times its cost of construction, and most companies, including the Great Western, had a market value that broadly matched but did not markedly exceed their cost.

Company	Cost	1844 value	Value as % of cost
London & Birmingham	£6,091,000	£13,378,000	220%
Great Western	£8,878,000	£8,890,000	101%
Liverpool & Manchester	£1,515,000	£3,410,000	225%
North Midland	£3,339,000	£3,100,000	93%
Eastern Counties	£2,778,000	£2,322,000	84%
Manchester & Birmingham	£1,910,000	£2,292,000	120%
London & Brighton	£2,621,000	£2,251,000	90%

Table 28: Market value of the principal railways, 1844

Dividend	Amount of capital (% of total)
15%	£256,000 (0.9%)
10%	£3,117,000 (11.6%)
6-7%	£5,703,500 (21.1%)
5-6%	£2,390,000 (8.9%)
4-5%	£5,027,000 (18.6%)
3-4%	£4,471,000 (16.6%)
2-3%	£4,049,000 (15%)
below 2%	£1,965,000 (7.3%)
Total	£26,978,500 (100%)

Table 29: Dividends paid on proportions of a total share capital of, 1844

The value of railway companies to shareholders lay both in the capital return they drew from their shares and the dividends those shares paid. The 1844 Select Committee set out an abstract of a return upon 36 of those it described as the 'principal' passenger railways, which had a combined route mileage of 1,356 miles. While these figures post-date the railway revolution, they do show the matured results of that revolution, not long after the explosion of railway incorporation had occurred. The Committee observed that their figures showed the average return on railway shares was 5.75 per cent, considerably in excess of contemporary bank interest rates and, at a time when there was no inflation, representing a very good return on investments. Table 29 sets out the total level of authorised capital paying the different levels of dividends given.

Despite this rate of return on investments in railways, the level of profits the railway companies were earning for their subscribers was not regarded as enormous; thus the 1844 Select Committee observed that it doubted

'...whether the establishment of railways in this country does not afford a more remarkable instance than can be cited ... [of] the almost uniform benefit to the public, combined with a very moderate standard of average remuneration to the projectors.'

CONCLUSION

Two factors, therefore, led to the different outcomes in 1834 and 1835, the failure then success of the Great Western incorporation Bills: first, the dropping of the plan for the 'divided route', and second, the employment of Osborne Ward to manage the Parliamentary process. Osborne Ward took the management of the political process out of the hands of Brunel, who had far too much to occupy himself in laying out a route and organising the locomotive stock of the Great Western, and into their more professional and more effective hands. The incorporation process confirms that while Brunel was an outstanding engineer, he was no politician and, indeed, he despised the need to compromise, which all who wish to succeed on the political stage have to accept. This not only caused the defeat of the 1834 Bill of incorporation, but was also to lead to the Great Western's failure in 1846 to prevent the Gauge Commission recommending that in future no new lines of railway should be authorised on Brunel's broad gauge. During the Committee stage in the House of Lords in 1835 Brunel was questioned hard about how the Great Western could have been established without either solicitors or a Company Secretary: it is clear from the fate of the 1834 Bill that this had been a grave error.

Yet despite this most unhelpful lack of sympathy for the demands of the political process, Brunel had achieved the foundation of the Great Western Railway. He had, like any genius, his detractors, but in its quality 'God's Wonderful Railway' rises above personal criticism, and still rightly holds the imagination of all lovers of railway history today.

APPENDIX 1
GREAT WESTERN CONSTITUENT COMPANIES FOUNDED BEFORE 1840

Birmingham, Bristol & Thames Junction [West London Railway]	21 June 1836
Bristol & Exeter	19 May 1836
Cheltenham & Great Western Union	21 June 1836
Chester & Birkenhead	12 July 1837
Duffryn, Llynvi & Porthcawl	10 June 1825
Forest of Dean [Bullo Railway Act]	10 June 1809
Great Western	31 August 1835
Hayle	27 June 1834
Liskeard & Looe	22 June 1825
Llanelly Railway & Dock	19 June 1828
Monmouthshire Railway & Canal [Monmouthshire Canal & Navigation Act]	3 June 1792
Park Mile (Newport) [Neutral Mile] [Monmouthshire Canal & Navigation Act]	30 June 1802
Rumney	20 May 1825
Stratford & Moreton	28 May 1821
Taff Vale	21 June 1836

APPENDIX 2
HISTORICAL MONEY VALUES

Year	Contemporary value	2001 value
1825	£1,000	£45,737
1830	£1,000	£53,322
1835	£1,000	£59,474
1840	£1,000	£47,357
1845	£1,000	£56,573

APPENDIX 3
BRUNEL'S RECOMMENDATION OF THE BROAD GAUGE TO HIS BOARD, 15 SEPTEMBER 1835

Upon the Great Western Railway, from Bristol to Bath, and from London to the Oxford Branch, a total distance of about 70 miles, including those portions upon which fully one-third of the traffic will take place, there will be no inclination exceeding four feet per mile, which will cause a resistance of only one pound and seven-tenths per ton, calling it even two pounds, while the friction is taken at 8 pounds, it appears that the latter will constitute 80% of the whole resistance. The importance of any improvement upon that which favours so large a proportion is obvious, but nevertheless, according to the present construction of railways, a limit has been put to this improvement, which limit is already reacted or at all events great impediments are thrown in the way of any material diminution of the friction, and this serious evil is produced indirectly by the width of the railways.

The resistance from friction is diminished as the proportion of the diameter of the wheel to that of the axle-tree is increased. There are some causes which, in practice, slightly influence this result, but within the limits of increase which could be required we may consider that practically the resistance from friction will be diminished exactly in the same ratio that the diameter of the wheel is increased. We have here, therefore, the means of materially diminishing this resistance.

The wheels upon railways were originally much smaller than they now are, as the speed has been increased and economy in power became more important, the diameters have been progressively increased and are now nearly double the size they were but a few years ago. Even upon the Liverpool & Manchester Railway I believe they have been increased nearly one-half, but by the present construction of the carriages they have reached their limit.

The width of the railway being only four feet 8 inches between the rails, or about four feet 6 inches between the wheels, the body of the carriage or the platform upon which the luggage is placed is of necessity extended over the tops of the wheels, and a space must also be left for the action of the springs of the carriage, and the load is raised unnecessarily high, while at the same time the size of the wheel is inconveniently limited.

If the centre of gravity of the load could be lowered, the motion would be more steady, and one of the causes of wear and tear both in rails and in carriages would be diminished. By simply widening the rails so that the body of the carriage might be kept entirely within the wheels, the centre of gravity might be considerably lowered and at the same time the diameter of the wheels is unlimited. I should propose 6 feet 10 inches to 7 feet as the width of the rails, which I think would admit of sufficient width of the carriage for all purposes. I am not prepared by any means at present to recommend any particular size of wheel, or even any great increase of the present dimensions. I believe they will be materially increased, but my great object would be in any possible way to render each part capable of improvement, and to remove what appears to be an obstacle to any great progress in such a very important point as the diameter of the wheels upon which the resistance, which governs the cost of transport and the speed that may be attained, so materially depends.

The objections which may be urged against these alterations are:

Firstly, the increased widths required in the cuttings, embankments and tunnels, and consequently the increased expenses;

Secondly, a greater amount of friction in the curves;

Thirdly, the additional weight of the carriages;

Fourthly, the inconvenience arising from the junction with the London & Birmingham Railway.

Firstly, as regards to the increase of the earth-work, bridges and tunnels, this would not be as great as would at first sight appear. The increased width of each railway does not effect the width between the rails on either side, as the total width of the bodies of the carriages remains the same, and as the slopes of the cuttings and embankments are the same, the total quantity would not necessarily be increased above a half, and the cost of the bridges and the tunnels would be augmented in about the same ratio, and such addition has been provided for in the estimates.

Secondly, the effect of the friction upon small curves. The necessary radius of curvature will be increased in the same ratio of the width between the wheel sizes at 5 to 7, but the portions of the total length which is curved to such a degree as to render this effect sensible is so small (not being above one and a half miles upon the whole Line, except immediately at the entrance of the depots) that it is not worth considering when a great advantage is to be gained upon the total distance of 120 miles.

Thirdly, the additional weight of the carriages. The axle-trees alone will be increased and they form but a small part of the total weight of the carriages. The frame will indeed be simplified and, I believe, this will fully counter-balance the increased length of axle-trees. If the wheels are materially increased in diameter, they must of course be stronger and consequently heavier. But this weight does not affect the friction at the axle-trees and not sensibly the resistance to traction, while their increased diameter affords the advantages which are sought for.

Fourthly, the inconvenience in effecting the junction with the London & Birmingham Railway. This I consider to be the only real obstacle to the adoption of the plan. One additional rail to each railway must be laid down. I do not foresee any great difficulty in doing this, but undoubtedly the London & Birmingham Railway Company may object to it. In that case, I see no remedy: the plan must be abandoned. It is therefore important that this point should be specially determined.

APPENDIX 4
SOURCE MATERIAL FOR THE
GREAT WESTERN RAILWAY

Original and new sources used for this book include the records of Parliamentary Select Committees on railway bills. These are manuscript summaries of what was said in Parliamentary Committees, contained in extremely tightly bound books slightly larger than A5 held by the House of Lords Record Office. These enable one to read the words of all the great men of the railway revolution of the 1830s – Brunel, Stephenson, Vignoles, Hudson, Locke – and many other less well-known people. However, the destruction of Parliament by fire in 1834 means that no Parliamentary accounts of the proceedings of the Select Committees on Bills to 1834 have survived, nor the text of Bills, which, because they did not receive the Royal Assent, were never printed. Fortunately, the Great Western, indignant at the defeat of its Bill in 1834, published its own summary of the Committee proceedings in Parliament.

Also used are Brunel's reports to the Great Western Board; the Board minutes of the Great Western, the Bristol & Exeter, the Cheltenham & Great Western Union, and other companies; contemporary Bristol newspapers; the accounts of the Great Western's solicitors in 1835; the private papers of the Earl of Carnarvon; reports of the company's performance supplied to Great Western proprietors' meetings; the Great Western's prospectuses and those of some other companies; the diary of George Gibbs, an early Great Western director; the papers of Sir Daniel Gooch, who played such an important role in making the Great Western one of the highest-quality railways in operation in Great Britain; the petitions to Parliament of the Great Western company and of various towns in support and opposition; the Great Western letterbook and that of the company's Secretary, Charles Saunders; papers held by the British Library relating to the questioning of the broad gauge by, principally, Liverpool proprietors; and the Sealed Register of Proprietors of 1835, enabling a picture to be drawn of the type of people who in 1835 bought Great Western shares, and where they lived. For reactions to the coming of the railways, the papers of Eton College provide much detail, as do those of Oxford University's Hebdomadal Board and the Earl of Carnarvon.

The Great Western Railway has attracted a larger secondary literature than any other single railway company. In the 1998 edition of his bibliography of British railway history, George Ottley lists 284 books and articles relating to the Great Western. However, he lists none for the London & Birmingham and only two for the Eastern Counties. For George Hudson's Midland Railway Ottley lists 129 books and articles.

Despite this vast secondary literature on the Great Western, its incorporation and its efforts to obtain Parliamentary sanction have been neglected. This is a gap in the literature on both the Great Western and early railways in general, and one that this book attempts to redress. One consequence has been the lack of appreciation of the significance in the 1830s of the development of railways in the modernisation of Parliament under the stress of the quantity of railway legislation with which it had to deal. Some consideration has been given by historians to the financing of the Great Western, in particular the sources of its capital.

All great men attract conflicting interpretations of the significance of their roles, as Brunel has from L. T. C. Rolt and from Adrian Vaughan. Much original source material, particularly the records of Parliament, emphasises the importance of Brunel in the incorporation and early development of the Great Western. A mass of outstanding source material for the early history of the Great Western exists.

APPENDIX 5
BIBLIOGRAPHY

(A) PRIMARY SOURCES

1. Documents relating to the Great Western Railway

Board Minutes (Public Record Office, RAIL250/1)

Minutes of Proprietors' Meetings (Public Record Office, RAIL 250/64)

Report of Directors to the First General Meeting of the Proprietors, 29 October 1835 (The Great Western Society, Swindon)

Company petition for the incorporation of the Great Western (Bristol Record Office, 17563 (1))

Petition of the inhabitants of Wells regarding the Great Western Bill, 1835 (Somerset County Record Office DD/FS 45/6/41)

Letter to Shareholders, explaining the loss of the 1834 Bill (Brunel Collection, Bristol University, DM305.III.5)

Sealed Register of the Proprietors of the Great Western Railway, 1835 (Public Record Office, RAIL251/1)

The 1821 Prospectus of a railway from Bristol to London (Public Record Office, RAIL253/663)

Report of the Committee on the Propriety of a Railway from Bristol to London (Brunel Collection, Bristol University DM306 III.3)

The two 1833 and the 1834 Prospectuses of the Great Western Railway (Public Record Office, RAIL253/63)

Great Western Railway Company prospectus, 1835 (Oriel College, Oxford)

Brunel's Reports to the Great Western Board (Public Record Office, RAIL250/82)

Carnarvon Papers, relating to the Earl of Carnarvon's negotiations over the sale of his land to the Great Western, 1835 (Highclere Castle, Box M)

Great Western Letterbook 1833 (Bristol Record Office, 12167.27)

Great Western Book of Reference (Bristol Record Office, 12167.27)

Osborne Ward account (Osborne Clarke, Bristol)

Charles Saunders's Letterbook (Public Record Office, RAIL253/106)

Letter from George Stephenson to the Directors of the Great Western Railway Company, 31 March, 1835 (Brunel Collection, University of Bristol, DM 306 II.9)

Report of Nicholas Wood and Sir John Hawkshaw to the Great Western's Board on the gauge of the Great Western, and Brunel's reply thereto (British Library, 8773 cc. 32)

Circular letter sent to prospective subscribers by Osborne Ward on the loss of the 1834 Bill (Gloucester Record Office JF 14.105 (14.25))

Circular letter sent to Members of Parliament on the introduction of the 1835 Great Western Bill to Parliament (Gloucester Record Office, Gloucester Collection 31 – 14.103.2)

2. Documents relating to the Bristol & Exeter Railway

Bristol & Exeter Board Minutes (Public Record Office RAIL75/1)

Bristol & Exeter Proprietors' Meetings' minutes (Public Record Office, RAIL75/49)

Petitions relating to the Bristol & Exeter Railway Bill, 1836 (Public Record Office, RAIL75/255)

3. Documents relating to the Cheltenham & Great Western Union

Cheltenham & Great Western Union Board Minutes (Public Record Office, RAIL 109/1)

4. Documents relating to other specific railways

(i) The Oxford & Great Western Union Railway

Oxford University Petition against the Oxford & Great Western Union Railway Bill, 1838 (Oxford University Archives, Bodleian Library, WPY22 (1S))

(ii) The London & Birmingham Railway

Prospectus of the London & Birmingham Railway 1833 (Eton College Library)

5. Parliamentary Documents and Accounts of Debate

May, Thomas Erskine *A Practical Treatise on the Law, Privileges, Proceedings and Usages of the House of Commons* (22nd Edition, London, 1997)

Speaker's Rules for the Hearing of Petitions by the Examiners, 18 November 1846

Hansard, Third Series, Vol 21

Mirror of Parliaments (House of Lords Record Office)

House of Commons Journals

House of Lords Journals

Dod's Parliamentary Companion (London, 1833)

Account of the Proceedings of the Great Western Railway Company, with Extracts from the Evidence given in support of the Great Western Bill before the Committee of the House of Commons in Session 1834 (Great Western Railway Society, Swindon)

Evidence to the House of Lords Committee on the Great Western Bill, 1835 Reports of Committees, Vol xxxix

Parliamentary Return of those spending over £2,000 on Railway Shares in 1845 (Accounts and Papers, 1846, Vol xxxviii)

Railway Returns, A Return of all moneys to be raised under the sanction of the Acts whereby railroad companies have been incorporated between the 1st day of January 1826 and the 1st day of January 1844 (House of Commons paper 1844 (No 159))

6. Parliamentary Select Committees and Royal Commissions

(All Commons Committees, unless specified as Lords Committees)

(i) On the subject of railways generally
Select Committee on Railways, 1839
   First Report (HC1839 (222) (X))
   Second Report (HC1839 (517) (X))
Select Committee on Railways, 1840
Select Committee on Railways, 1844
   First Report (HC1844 (37) (XI))
   Second Report (HC1844 (79) (XI))
   Third Report (HC1844 (166) (XI))
   Fourth Report (HC1844 (283) (XI))
   Fifth Report (HC1844 (318) (XI)) (Gladstone's Committee)
   Sixth Report (HC1844 (324) (XI))
The House of Lords Committee on Compensation, 1845 (Lords Sessional Papers, 1845, Vol xviii
   [27])
The Select Committee on Railway Acts Enactments, 1846
House of Lords Select Committee on Railways, 1846 (Lords Sessional Papers, Vol xxxvi)
The Select Committee on Railways and Canals Amalgamations, Second Report 6 May 1846
The Gauge Commission (House of Commons Paper 1846 (34))
The Select Committee on Private Bills, Third Report 21 July 1847

(ii) Select Committees on specific railways
Great Western Company reprint of the Commons proceedings on the 1834 Bill (Great Western
   Railway Society, Swindon)
Great Western Railway Bill 1835 (House of Commons evidence, 1835, Vol 4)
Great Western Railway Bill 1837 (Reports from Committees, Vol 14)
London & Birmingham Railway Bill 1832 (House of Lords Committee, 1832)
Midland Counties Railway Bill, 18 March 1836
North Midland Railway Bill, 16 March 1836 (Vol 32)
Oxford & Great Western Union Railway Bill (Commons evidence, 1838, Vol 2)
York & North Midland Railway Bill, 1836 (Vol 40)

7. Acts of the principal railway companies to 1840
Bristol and Exeter Railway
6 W4, cap 36, 1836
1 Vict, cap 26, 1838
3 Vict, cap 47, 1840

Eastern Counties Railway
6 & 7 W4, cap 196, 1836
2 Vict, cap 81, 1838
4 Vict, cap 14, 1840

Great Western Railway
5 & 6 W4, cap 107, 1835
6 W4, cap 77, 1836
2 Vict, cap 27, 1839

London & Birmingham Railway
3 W4, cap 36, 1833
5 & 6 W4, cap 56, 1835
1 Vict, cap 64, 1837
2 Vict, cap 39, 1839

London & Brighton Railway
5 W4, cap 10, 1835
6 & 7 W4, cap 121, 1836
1 Vict, cap 20, 1838
2 Vict, cap 1, 1840

Manchester & Birmingham Railway
1 Vict, cap 69, 1837

North Midland Railway
6 & 7 W4, cap 107, 1835

8. Newspapers
Berkshire Gazette
Bristol Gazette
Bristol Mercury
The Chronicle (Reading)
The Mercury (Reading)
The Times

9. Miscellaneous original sources
Clyde Navigation Trust Annual Accounts (Glasgow City Archives, TCN6/1/1)

10. Published memoirs
Simmons, Jack (ed) *The Birth of the Great Western Railway; Extracts from the Diary and Correspondence of George Henry Gibbs* (Bath, 1971)
Wilson, R. B. (ed) *Memoirs and Diary of Sir Daniel Gooch* (Newton Abbot, 1972)

(B) SECONDARY SOURCES

Adams, William (ed) *Encyclopedia of the Great Western Railway* (Sparkford, 1993)
Barnes, E. G. *The Rise of the Midland Railway* (London, 1966)
Barnes, Thomas *History of the Commerce and Town of Liverpool* (Liverpool, 1852)
Bond, Maurice F. *Guide to the Records of Parliament* (London, 1971)
Boyce, Benjamin *The Benevolent Man: a Life of Ralph Allen* (Harvard, 1967)
Boyes, Graham, et al *Ottley's Bibliography of British Railway History, Second Supplement, 12957-19605* (York, 1998)
Broadbridge, Seymour *Studies in Railway Expansion and the Capital Market in England, 1825-1875* (London, 1970)
Brunel, I. [Jnr] *Life of I. K. Brunel* (London, 1870)
Bryan, Tim *The Golden Age of the Great Western Railway* (London, 1991)

Paddington: Great Western Gateway (Wadenhoe, 1997)

Brunel, The Great Engineer (Shepperton, 2000)

Buchanan, Angus *Brunel – The Life and Times of Isambard Kingdom Brunel* (London, 2002)

Carlson, Robert E. *The Liverpool & Manchester Railway Project, 1821-1831* (Newton Abbot, 1969)

Cattell, John and Falconer, Keith *Swindon: the Legacy of a Railway Town* (London, 1995)

Channon, Geoffrey *Bristol and the Promotion of the Great Western Railway* (Bristol, 1995)

The Recruitment of Directors to the Board of the Great Western (Journal of Transport History, 3rd series, Vol 7, No 1, 1996)

Chapman, W. G. *The Cornish Riviera Limited* (London, 1936)

Clew, Kenneth R. *The Kennet & Avon Canal*, 2nd edition (Newton Abbot, 1973)

Concise Dictionary of National Biography (Oxford, 1996)

Dalby, L. J. *The Wilts & Berks Canal* (Lingfield, 1971)

Donaghy, Thomas *Liverpool & Manchester Railway Operations 1831-1845* (Newton Abbot, 1972)

Francis, J. A. *A History of the English Railway: its Social Relations and Revelations, 1820-1845* (London, 1851, reprinted Newton Abbot)

Gale, P. R. *The Great Western Railway* (1926, reprinted Weston-super-Mare, 1986)

Galt, William *Railway Reform: Expediency and Practicability considered* (Bodleian Pamphlet, 44.1640)

Griffiths, Denis *Locomotive Engineers of the GWR* (Wellingborough, 1987)

Hatfield, Charles *British Canals* (Newton Abbot, 1974)

Jeans, J. S. *A History of the Stockton & Darlington Railway* (London, 1875, reprinted Newcastle-upon-Tyne, 1975)

Jones, Gwyn Briwnant and Dunstone, Denis *The Origins of the LMS in South Wales* (Llandysul, 1999)

Joy, David *Regional History of the Railways of Great Britain, Vol 8, South and West Yorkshire* (London, 1984)

Kostal, R. W. *Common Law, Common Lawyers, and the English Railway Industry, 1830-89* (Oxford University, D Phil thesis, 1989)

Laing, W. S. *Railway Taxation* (London, 1849)

Lambert, Richard S. *The Railway King: A Study of George Hudson and the Business Morals of his Times* (2nd impression, London, 1964)

Little, Bryan *The City and County of Bristol: A Study of Atlantic Civilisation* (London, 1954, reprinted Wakefield, 1967)

MacDermot, E. T., rev Clinker, C. R. *History of the Great Western Railway*, Vol 1 (first revised edition, London, 1964)

Neal, Sheila *All Change for Slough* (*Backtrack*, Vol 13, No 1)

Norris, John *The Stratford & Moreton Tramway* (Guildford, 1987)

Peacock, A. J. *George Hudson, 1800-1871, The Railway King* (York, 1986)

Pember-Reeves, W. *English Railways; their Development and their Relation to the State* (London, 1915)

Philips, Daphne *How the Great Western came to Berkshire: a Railway History 1833-1882* (Reading, 1975)

Pollins, Harold *The Finance of the Liverpool & Manchester Railway* (*Economic History Review*, 2nd Series, Vol v, No 1)

Porter, George *The Progress of the Nation* (London, 1851)

Pugsley, Alfred *The Works of Isambard Kingdom Brunel* (Bristol, 1976)

Reed, M. V. C. *Investment in Railways in Britain, 1820-1844* (Oxford, 1975)

Reid, Helen *Bristol & Co, The History of Bristol's long-running Businesses, 1710 to the present day* (Bristol, 1987)

Ridsdale, J. H. & G. *The Prices of Shares in Canals, and Railways, share brokers of Albion Street, Leeds, 29 May 1841* (Bodleian Library, 247917C77 (1))

Rolt, L. T. C. *Isambard Kingdom Brunel* (London, 1957)

Rosevear, Alan *Response of the Turnpikes to the coming of the Railway – the extension of the Great Western Railway to Steventon & Oxford* (private publication, Wantage, revised edition 1994)

Salt, Samuel *Facts and Figures principally relating to Railways and Commerce* (London, 1848)

Scrivenor, Harry *The Railways of the United Kingdom Statistically Considered* (London, 1849)

Sekon, G. A. *History of the Great Western Railway* (2nd edition, London, 1895)

Shepton, Robert *The Defeat of the Oxford & Great Western Union Railway Bill 1837* (*Journal of the Railway and Canal Historical Society*: Part 1, No 170; Part 2, No 173; Part 3, No 176

Simmons, Jack *The Railways of Britain* (London, 1986)
>> *St Pancras Station* (London, 1968)
>> *The Railway in Town and Country, 1830-1914* (London, 1986)
>> *The Victorian Railway* (London, 1995)

Simmons, Jack and Biddle, Gordon *Oxford Companion to British Railway History* (Oxford, 1997)

South, Raymond *Crown, College and Railways: how the Railways came to Eton* (London, 1978)

Tuck, Henry *The Railway Shareholders' Manual* (London, 1845)

Vaughan, Adrian *Isambard Kingdom Brunel, Engineering Knight-Errant* (London, 1991)
>> *Railwaymen, Politics and Money* (London, 1997)
>> *Brunel – Fads and Fallacies* ('North Star', Newsletter of the Friends of Swindon Railway Museum, Vol 5, No 6, autumn 2001)

Ward, J. R. *The Finance of Canal Building in Eighteenth Century England* (Oxford, 1976)

Webster, N. W. *Joseph Locke, Railway Revolutionary* (London, 1970)

Whittle, G. *The Newcastle & Carlisle Railway* (Newton Abbot, 1979)

Williams, Archibald *Brunel and After* (London, 1925)

Williams, Frederick S. *The Midland Railway: its Rise and Progress* (London, 1878)
>> *Our Iron Roads* (London, 1852)

Williams, O. Cyprian *The Historical Development of Private Bill Procedure and the Standing Orders of the House of Commons* 2 Vols (London, 1948-9)

Woodward, Llewellyn *The Age of Reform, England 1815-70* (2nd edition, Oxford, 1992)

www.dataconversion 2002 – web site giving conversion figures for money values

INDEX